PRAISE FOR
IDEAS ON A DEADLINE

Phil Cooke doesn't pull any punches when it comes to helping creative thinkers maximize their creative output. Brilliantly honest, insightful, informative, and entertaining, this is the book guaranteed to help anyone trying to come up with ideas in this crazy, chaotic, work-from-home world. I've been doing creative advertising for almost forty years—but *Ideas on a Deadline* has given me the kind of practical advice I wish I had learned decades ago.

—Craig Murray
Founder, CEO of MOCEAN, 3-Time North American
"Entertainment Advertising Agency of the Year"

The only reason I was able to write this endorsement was because Phil gave me a deadline! Once again, Phil has delivered a pithy and profound mix of hard-earned wisdom and hilarious anecdotes. This is a piquant reminder that the world is rife with creatives wracked with anxiety, and the answer to the riddle of inspiration is always, inevitably, to do. So keep a pad nearby when reading this, so the spigot of imagination that *Ideas on a Deadline* opens will have a beautiful bucket to fill. Peace.

—Todd Komarnicki
Producer *Elf*, Writer *Sully*, and deadline-meeter *always*

Producing television and film projects around the world, we understand the pressure of deadlines more than most people—and that's why Phil's book is so important. Anyone who's creative (no matter what business you're in) needs to read it. It's a masterclass on how to develop amazing ideas under pressure, and it will change your perspective on creativity.

—Roma Downey and Mark Burnett

Phil Cooke is one of my favorite people and a dear friend. He has perfected the art of delivering wisdom, insight, and common sense with just the right amount of humor to make it all stick. It's no surprise that

Ideas on a Deadline is packed with practical ways to help you achieve maximum productivity and maintain your creative spark.

—Bobby Gruenewald
Founder/CEO, YouVersion & Pastor/Innovation Leader, Life.Church
Named to *Fast Company's* list of the Most Creative People in Business

Ideas on a Deadline is full of insights born of Phil's reflection on his own long and successful career. I've been an actor for forty-plus years, and in my world, we film on Friday, we open on the sixteenth, and dress rehearsal is Thursday. No excuses, no extensions, no "my dog ate my homework." Everything Phil says makes sense to me. I was once so desperate to find a character a few days before the final dress that I did all the scenes in different cartoon voices, just to shake something loose. (Luckily, it worked.) Yes, it was a bad idea, but it was an idea! And I learned something Phil emphasizes: don't wait for a great idea; just have a lot of ideas and pick the best one. *Ideas on a Deadline* is not a step-by-step one-size-fits-all. It's a useful, practical guide on crossing the threshold from imagination to creation.

—Fred Applegate
Actor, TV, Broadway, and London: *The Producers, Wicked,*
Young Frankenstein, The Last Ship, The Ferryman

I have to be honest. I may end up inadvertently stealing a ton of the insights I found in *Ideas on a Deadline* and passing them along as brilliant advice to other creatives. But in fairness, I'll also wholeheartedly recommend that every creative—young and old—read this enlightening and encouraging book. It's not just about deadlines. It's about the power we have as creatives to understand, influence, and unleash our own creativity.

—Danny Bryan
Advertising Creative Director, TRG

As a production accountant and finance executive, my world is all about the deadlines and the numbers. It's easy to get lost in the debits and credits, but Phil's book reminds us that there is creativity in every line of work, and it provides the steps needed to regain creativity while not losing productivity. The truth is, we're all creatives. And this perspective has changed the way I approach budgeting, tracking, and managing films and teams worldwide. I highly recommend *Ideas on a Deadline* to anyone who wants to make a change or needs a boost of creativity in their everyday work life.

—Kimberly Robinson
Finance Executive, 20th Century Studios, Hulu, Disney

PHIL COOKE

"Phil's book is so important. It's a masterclass on how to develop amazing ideas under pressure and it will change your perspective on creativity."

MARK BURNETT AND ROMA DOWNEY

IDEAS ON
A
DEADLINE

HOW TO BE CREATIVE
WHEN THE CLOCK IS TICKING

INSPIRE

Cover design by: Eric Powell
Cover Photo by: Steve Anderson Photography

ISBN: 978-1-957369-04-4   1 2 3 4 5 6 7 8 9 10

Printed in the United States of America

DEDICATION

This book is dedicated to our young grandchildren Kennady and Clyde.

I never cease to be amazed at their imaginations as they see so much for the first time. They challenge my own creativity (and patience) every day and inspire me to keep seeing the world in new ways.

This book is for you.

CONTENTS

PART IV. THE MOMENTUM

Creativity is a quality we all admire, but
sometimes don't understand.
Can you study creativity?
Should you monetize it?
What is creativity, anyway, and why does it matter in a
world of robotics, quantum computing, and AI?
The answer, we believe, is that creativity is at
the fundamental heart of all that we do.
It's what makes us human, artistic, emotional
(and sometimes destructive) beings.
Creativity can generate wealth as well as joy,
and there has never been a better time to be creative.
—Darius Sanai, editor in chief, *LUX* magazine

Some of the best work out there has been produced with an impending deadline.
—Justin Ruben, group creative director, *Droga5*

13

YOU HAVE AN HOUR TO REWRITE EVERYTHING

We are always thinking about our art and work, but when we are under a little more pressure, I think that we just naturally step into overdrive, and our creative muscles start to flex . . . so in these moments of pressure, we find ourselves creating some of our best work!

—Cheryl Family, SVP, brand strategy
+ creative, Viacom Catalyst

Early in my career, I was living in the Midwest and desperately looking for a bridge to Hollywood. I had worked in Los Angeles, California, for a year after college, but that was back in the days before independent film and TV production became commonplace. Pretty much the only chance of getting in the door at that time was through a union, and if you didn't have a relative in one already, you were out of luck. So, after working as a production assistant, assistant camera operator, assistant director, assistant editor, and assistant anything else I could find on a succession of educational films, religious programs, and forgettable local advertising, I went back to the Midwest because I had just gotten married, and I needed a regular job.

Years later, a big opportunity happened when producer Marty Krofft along with his brother Sid launched a new prime time series on network television. Krofft, long known for legendary children's programming like *H.R. Pufnstuf* and *Sigmund and the Sea Monsters*, was moving into prime time with a bang. At the time, he was producing a new series of TV specials featuring Barbara Mandrell and the Mandrell sisters and now was launching a completely new program.

Sid and Marty were big time.

I'd been writing and producing a lot of television commercials, so through a mutual connection, Marty reached out to me to write and produce a series of TV spots to promote the new show. He asked me to write three scripts and bring them to his office in Hollywood to discuss the campaign. I knew this was a big step for me and couldn't afford to blow the opportunity.

After writing the scripts, I boarded a plane to Los Angeles knowing this would be a very consequential meeting. I rented a car and drove to what was then Sunset Gower Studios in Hollywood. While I had been involved in television production for years by then, I quickly realized I was now in a completely different world. This was prime time network television. Walking into the production offices, you could see the excitement and pressure involved in producing a major TV series, but if that weren't intimidating enough, I discovered Marty had about eight secretaries and personal assistants. I quietly threaded my way past all their desks and was ushered into his office where I introduced myself and set the scripts on his desk.

He didn't ask me to sit down.

He read over the scripts, set them back down on his desk, looked up at me, and said, "This is shit. This is absolute shit. I can't believe I brought you all the way out here to give me this junk." Then he paused, and I worried his assistants might have overheard the noise my heart made when it dropped to the floor. I was devastated. I went from pure elation to complete failure in about two minutes. I started thinking about when the next flight home was leaving LAX.

After a pause that seemed like hours, he said, "But I've heard about you, and I've heard you're better than this. I'll tell you what; I have to go check on a recording session for a new album. While I'm gone, there's a conference room at the other end of the office. My assistants outside will get you anything you need—typewriter, pens, notepads, coffee, a sandwich, whatever. But when I come back in an hour, I expect to see three new scripts."

With that, he got up and walked out of the room.

I made my way to the conference room in a fog. His secretary assembled what I needed and shut the door, and I sat there in complete silence wondering what to do. He had given me a second chance, but I had already done what I thought was my best work. So what do I do now?

I only had an hour, and the clock was ticking.

I sat there staring at the typewriter (this was before I could afford a laptop), and I started to choke. After all, I'd spent weeks working on the original scripts, and now he was giving me an hour—maybe less? The pressure and urgency of the moment rushed in, and I almost got up and walked back to my rental car.

But I started writing.

I was determined not to use a single word of the old scripts and create something entirely new. I don't remember much after that because the rest of the hour became a blur until one of his older, rather gruff secretaries poked her head in the door.

"Mr. Krofft would like to see the new scripts."

I pulled the last page out of the typewriter and walked back to his office. Thinking back, I probably looked like I could have starred in the movie *Dead Man Walking*. I felt okay about the scripts, but after all, I had felt *good* about the first version, and he hated them, so who knew what he'd think? I reenacted the earlier visit. I walked in and set the scripts on his desk.

He didn't invite me to sit down this time either.

Marty read the scripts, put them down, and looked back up at me. "Now *this* is what I'm talking about. This is good. We can make this work."

I thought I might faint. We shook hands, he invited me to hang around the set for a couple of days to meet the team, took me to a few restaurants and clubs on Sunset Boulevard, and a friendship began that opened the door to doing more TV writing, as well as meeting entertainment professionals that I've worked with many times since.

Looking back later, I realized that experience of delivering a completely new set of commercial scripts inside an hour forced me to understand that creativity isn't about waiting for inspiration, hearing from a muse, or having a "eureka" moment. Creativity isn't mystical, weird, or illusive; it's simply solving a problem on a deadline.

And since that time, I've dissected my experience in that conference room over and over in my mind, and I know beyond a shadow of a doubt that it can be replicated and used anytime you're up against a wall. Writing the first draft of those scripts had taken weeks because I wanted them to be absolutely perfect. I didn't rush things, and I had waited for the creative muse to hit, but that method had let me down. Marty was right. While he was more verbally explicit than I, the original scripts deserved the trash can. But with an hour deadline, the pressure of a network TV show, and standing on the brink of a do-or-die moment, the ideas showed up.

WHAT HAPPENED IN THAT CONFERENCE ROOM?

The kind of experience that happened in that room is what this book is about. Since that time, I've had thousands of similar experiences writing, producing, running film and television productions—all with budgets and deadlines. Chances are you're not that different. You may work in a different field, but whether you're a filmmaker, designer, coach, teacher, real estate agent, or a company or nonprofit leader, your budget is limited, and a deadline is looming.

True creativity—especially at a high level—isn't easy, but if you're willing to understand it, prepare for it, and activate it in your life, there's no end to what's possible. This book is about delivering great ideas on a deadline. Hopefully, it will forever dispel the myth that truly creative people must wait for a moment of inspiration before they start a project.

Your days of waiting are over. Now it's time to create!

19

INTRODUCTION

THE CREATIVE DEMAND

> *The economic need for creativity has registered itself in the rise of a new class, which I call the Creative Class. Some 38 million Americans, 30 percent of all employed people, belong to this new class. I define the core of the Creative Class to include people in science and engineering, architecture and design, education, arts, music and entertainment, whose economic function is to create new ideas, new technology, and/or new creative content.*
>
> —Richard Florida, *The Rise of the Creative Class*

A lthough I've worked closely with hundreds of creative artists over my career and served on the board of a highly respected literary journal, I've always considered my personal and professional creative work more in the artisan category. There's little point in quibbling about the definition of artist versus artisan, but I've always thought in terms of an artisan being someone who does creative work for a purpose or function.

In other words, an *artisan* creates something specific and (hopefully) gets paid for it.

On the other hand, while many creative *artists* get paid (some very well), an artist is more likely to create for the work itself, whether or not it has a functional purpose.

No matter how highly you regard your work, vision, or creative calling, for the purposes of this book, I would encourage you to begin thinking like an artisan. Whether you're a filmmaker, writer, graphic designer, athletic coach, realtor, hair stylist, business or nonprofit leader, pastor, teacher—or whatever you do—I'm betting you have to come up with creative solutions on a regular basis. In most cases, those creative challenges have a deadline, and at some point, must produce results.

> **This book is about how to raise your game when it comes to meeting those deadlines without losing any of your creativity—or sanity—in the process.**

In my career, I've written and produced countless television programs, documentary films, short videos, TV commercials, magazine articles, blog posts, and this will be my tenth book (not counting the two at the start when I was hired as a ghostwriter for someone else). Although most would call me a television *producer,* I've also written and directed nearly everything I've ever produced.

Two things are important about that work:

1) **I get paid for it.** Our team at Cooke Media Group is a client-driven media production company, and while we produce many of our own in-house projects, we're also hired to tell our clients' stories.

2) **Every project has a deadline.** While I would love to sit by my patio firepit until the muse hits me and creative fire falls from heaven, nearly all my projects have due dates, and those deadlines can rarely be changed. When a television program is scheduled for broadcast on a network or streaming platform, you just can't call and ask for a few more days. In a similar way, TV commercials are the point of the spear for other national advertising campaigns, and their delivery dates are usually set in stone. The Super Bowl won't change its date because I haven't come up with a good enough idea for a spot.

If I don't deliver, I'm out of business.

A WORLD OF ACCELERATING CHANGE

Years ago, I wrote a book called *Jolt! Get the Jump on a World That's Constantly Changing*. It was created to help people navigate the accelerating change I saw coming in the culture—change that is now playing out before our eyes. And as the world accelerates, demand for creative work grows and is more likely to have deadlines attached.

Mobile devices are updated on a yearly basis, and for a designer, engineer, or programmer not to make that deadline would hold back billion-dollar tech giants—not to mention millions of disappointed customers. Movies and TV series are in constant pipelines for various streaming services. Athletic coaches face locked-in schedules, evolving game plans, coaching styles, and playoffs, and the demands grow year by year. The business world evolves and culture changes. The world is accelerating, and creative thinking must accelerate with it.

At the same time, we're experiencing more distractions than ever. The constant flood of emails, text messages, phone calls, social media, and other messages are overwhelming us. So when we do face a creative challenge, we must fight what writer Steven Pressfield calls "The Resistance." In his book *The War of Art* he says: "It's not the writing part that's hard. What's hard is sitting down to write. What keeps us from sitting down is Resistance."[1]

The bottom line is that high-level creativity is challenging enough. But we're also trying to be creative during a time when there is higher demand for creative results, there are more distractions, and those results have to be better than ever.

SING ALONG WITH MITCH AND THE POWER OF A DEADLINE

I remember when legendary conductor and musician Mitch Miller died at age ninety-nine. He was a very successful music producer but will probably be best known for hosting the musical TV series *Sing Along with Mitch*. All of us Baby Boomers grew up with it. Along with major stars he produced in his lifetime, one of the most interesting stories is about Johnny Mathis. After numerous best-selling albums with Johnny, Mitch had to fulfill a last contract, but as the deadline approached, he had no material for the album. Desperate to come up with something, he decided to go back and pull the best-selling songs from Johnny's career. He called it *Johnny's Greatest Hits*. It turned out to be a blockbuster. In fact, it was so successful that it stayed on the charts for ten years! That was the first "greatest hits" album, and of course, it started a huge industry. Mitch was a musical genius and one of the great showmen of his generation. But it's possible his greatest idea only happened because his back was against the wall, and a deadline was looming.

Next time you face a deadline, stop looking at it as an obstacle, and think of it as a potential springboard to what could be the greatest idea of your life.

The other day my wife, Kathleen, and I were in the car listening to a new "Beatles" channel on satellite radio. She remarked on the amazing

---

1   Steven Pressfield, *The War of Art* (London: Orion, 2003).

number of songs the Beatles had obviously recorded that we'd never heard before, and honestly, a significant number of those songs are junk. The Beatles literally transformed rock and roll, and we've come to think that everything they recorded was brilliant. But the truth is—even with the greatest artists—quantity comes before quality.

With the exception of only a handful of artists (although we don't know how much material artists like Shakespeare tossed in the trash or has been lost), the vast majority of creative geniuses had to learn the craft. And in that process, they created a lot of forgettable work.

To get great ideas, you need lots of ideas.

The point is, don't assume your first screenplay, novel, song, or other work is the big one. I met someone new to Hollywood recently who told me he was a screenwriter.

"What have you written?" I asked.

His reply? "One screenplay, and I'm trying to sell that."

Good luck.

Most successful writers have boxes full of screenplays, novels, notes, aborted projects and more that they would be embarrassed to show anyone. But all that work was a training camp—the roadmap that got them to where they are now.

So when it comes to creativity and developing ideas, just do the work, and worry later about what's good and what isn't. Because that's what it takes to get from where you are to where you want to be.

To mine for diamonds, you have to dig through a lot of dirt.

IDEAS ON A DEADLINE

A CONFESSION

I should start this book with a confession: I love deadlines. After thousands of creative challenges, I don't even get excited about a project until I see the deadline looming in the distance. I've had airline pilots tell me that a take-off can be rather routine until they see the end of the runway speeding toward the plane. That's when the blood starts pumping, the adrenaline starts flowing, and the mind sharpens.

I'm not sure if terror is part of the equation or not, but there's no question that over my career writing books, producing television programming, advertising, blog posts, podcasts, and more—deadlines motivate me more than anything else.

And yet, I constantly meet creative people who find deadlines absolutely paralyzing. They have become so afraid of any kind of schedule that they actually turn down amazing projects simply because they refuse to face the end of the runway. They may be waiting for inspiration from above, the muse to hit, or perhaps a eureka moment, but whatever it is, it's holding them back.

IS IT MAGIC?

There are plenty of wonderful books on creativity out there, but this isn't one of them. This book is about making breakthrough ideas happen under the pressure of a deadline. And for what it's worth, I've discovered there is absolutely no need to lower your creative excellence just because time is running out, and you need to deliver.

Perhaps, more importantly, I'm not talking about a *secret formula* or *hidden key*. This isn't magic. You can't just call great ideas into existence when you need them. However, you *can* grease the wheel. This book is about proven techniques that plenty of other creative professionals and I have used to help rev up the process—particularly when you're under the gun.

If that's you, then you're in the right place. From this point on, we're going to figure out how to make creative ideas show up when you need them most.

I've divided up the book into four key sections:

1) The Mindset
2) The Motivation
3) The Method
4) The Momentum

We'll start with what I call the creative *mindset*—how we need to reset our thinking for tackling great creative challenges. We'll discuss the role passion plays in creativity, why deadlines matter, and the real truth about having eureka moments.

Then we'll explore the *motivation* behind great ideas—how to build confidence in your creative abilities, how to open up space in your day for new ideas, dealing with fear, and how to look at challenges with a fresh vision.

The main section of the book will focus on the *method*. This is where the rubber meets the road and covers how to use creative extensions and get clarity. It ends with a list of techniques I've discovered that will help breakthrough ideas happen when the pressure is on.

Finally, we look to the future and discuss your *momentum*. Where do you go from here? As you become more comfortable with creating ideas on a deadline, how do you become a creative leader? How do you inspire other creative people? We'll discuss designing an atmosphere for creativity, secrets for leading high achievers, and how to take your creativity to the next level in your career.

I would encourage you to not skip around, but read the book straight through. There's a method to the madness, and I want you to understand the foundation before we start building the house.

And that starts with a creative mindset.

PART 1
THE MINDSET
THE ART OF FOCUSING ON WHAT MATTERS

*You don't know what it is to stay a whole day
with your head in your hands trying to squeeze
your unfortunate brain so as to find a word.*

—**Gustave Flaubert, novelist**

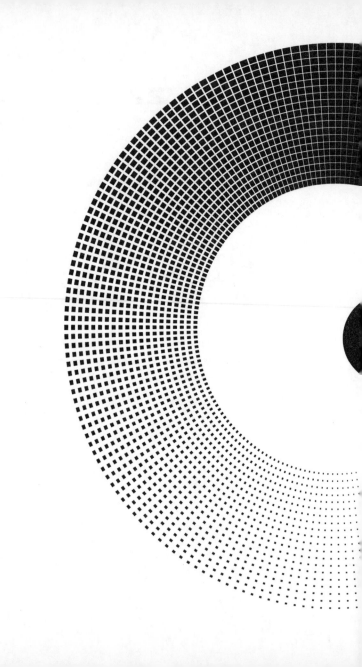

CHAPTER 1

NEVER MISS A DEADLINE

I am a person who works well under pressure.
In fact, I work so well under pressure that at times,
I will procrastinate in order to create this pressure.

—**Stephanie Pearl-McPhee, author**

Before we become brilliant under pressure, there are a few background principles that are important to establish. The first is understanding the *discipline* involved in the creative act.

You can be as creative as you want to be and take all the time you need if you're sitting on your back porch painting watercolors or writing and self-publishing your own book. But if you're using your creativity in the service of clients, a great cause, or bigger purpose, you'll soon be bumping up against two gigantic issues: *budgets and deadlines*. As foot soldiers of creativity, we like to make jokes about it, and one of my favorites is the classic Douglas Adams quote: "I love deadlines. I like the whooshing sound they make as they fly by."

Playwright Tony Kushner, discussing his creative process has said, "I work best after the deadline has passed, when I'm in a panic." Whatever your perspective on deadlines, the reality is that in a creative environment, *results matter*. Advertising legend David Ogilvy is famous for saying, "It's not creative unless it sells." That's a hard thing to digest for young creatives, but particularly here in Hollywood, no matter how creative a designer gets with a movie poster concept, or a director gets with a film, or a producer gets with mixing a hit song, if it doesn't deliver, it's tough to make a comeback.

Years ago, I consulted with a nonprofit organization whose creative team was only interested in being as imaginative as possible. They produced some amazing work in the process, but it never moved the needle for the organization. Because they weren't willing to have a disciplined approach to strategy, goals, and outcomes, everything they created was fun and creative, but it all ultimately failed. They wanted to have a creative *party*, but the organization needed *results*.

> *The absence of limitations is the enemy of art.*
> —ORSON WELLES, DIRECTOR OF *CITIZEN KANE*

That's why discipline matters in creativity. Finding the right time of day to create, the right place, and the right tools are paramount to achieving your best results. But the ultimate question is this:

How much can you shake up traditional thinking while on a budget and while facing a hard deadline?

It's interesting to note that in almost every case, when a filmmaker here in Hollywood gets complete control and an unlimited budget, the project invariably fails. There seems to be something about having hard rails on the sides of the bowling alley that actually inspires creativity.

Christopher Nolan? Quentin Tarantino? Steven Spielberg? Martin Scorsese? All deal with budgets and deadlines. So my advice is to stop fighting the limitations, and start using those boundaries to shake things up. Just a change in that perception alone will unleash a new attitude and perspective on your work.

After all, we're talking about creativity, right? We're talking about the ability to break through. That's why it's encouraging to remember the quote by advertising maven George Lois: "Creativity can solve almost any problem. The creative act, the defeat of habit by originality, overcomes everything."

Set a deadline. The earlier the better.
—CHRISTOPHER COX, AUTHOR OF *THE DEADLINE EFFECT*

Historically, the concept of a deadline was the "deadline" surrounding a military prison or stockade. Step beyond that line, and a prisoner would be shot on sight—no questions asked. Writing in his Civil War diary in 1863, Robert Ransom said:

> *Before noon we were turned into the pen which is merely enclosed by a ditch and the dirt taken from the ditch thrown up on the outside, making a sort of breastwork. The ditch serves as a dead line, and no prisoners must go near the ditch.*[2]

In his *History of the Great Rebellion*, Thomas Prentice Kettell described in 1866 a memorial for President Lincoln attributed by Union officers posted in Charleston referencing Confederate prisoners:

> *They are fast losing hope and becoming utterly reckless of life. Numbers, crazed by their sufferings, wander about in a state of*

---

2 "The Bloody History of 'Deadline,'" *Merriam-Webster*, https://www.merriam-webster.com/words-at-play/your-deadline-wont-kill-you.

> *idiocy. Others deliberately cross the 'Dead Line' and are remorse-*
> *lessly shot down.*[3]

Later it evolved to the printing press and became the point in time after which no more type could be set, and the printing process started. Eventually, a deadline became the date or time a story, manuscript, or article was due.

While looming deadlines can terrify creative people, over and over in my career, I've seen how they can also achieve remarkable results. In fact, even in the cases of creative people who routinely miss deadlines, I've discovered that simply giving them a false deadline earlier on the calendar often solves the problem.

And today, more and more research indicates the positive aspects of good deadlines. However, most creatives will simply delay until the last minute resulting in rushed, incomplete, or less than perfect work.

The challenge becomes *managing* deadlines, and understanding how you personally react, deal with, and accept deadlines can be the key to a long creative career. So just in case you're hearing otherwise, *deadlines matter*, and they matter for a lot of reasons. Here are just a few:

1) **When you miss a deadline, you're telling your employer or clients that their priorities don't matter.** You're sending them the message that your time is more important than their projects. Even if it is more important, that's not a perception you want them to have. After all, if you convey your time is more important than their projects, then they'll find someone else who appreciates them more.

2) **You're sending your employer or client a message that you're not organized.** If you can't hit a deadline, then something's wrong. Either you're incompetent or don't know how to schedule your time. Either way, that's not someone with whom they want to be in business.

---

3 Thomas Prentice Kettell, *History of the Great Rebellion* (Hartford: L. Stebbins, 1866).

3) **Finally, it undermines your credibility.** Hey—you promised that you'd hit the deadline, and when you don't, it makes you a liar, plain and simple.

Here's the bottom line:

Sure, there are a million reasons (some actually legitimate) that cause you to be late delivering on a project. But being late is not a good thing. If you know it's going to happen, here's my advice:

1) **Don't commit to the deadline.** The truth is, your good intentions don't matter. All that matters is hitting the deadline. If you can't do that, you're toast. So don't promise what you know you can't deliver.

2) **Let the client know the minute (or second) you realize you'll be late.** I had one video editor who was terrified to tell me he wasn't going to make the deadline. So, project after project, he'd wait until the last minute to break the news. Problem was, at the last minute, it was too late for me to do anything about it, so he put me in a very difficult spot. Tell the client the minute you can't make it, so he or she can make alternative plans. Believe me, they'll have a much better feeling for you than if you leave them hanging.

3) **The best answer? Hit the *&%$ deadline.** If it weren't critical, the employer or client wouldn't have given it to you. I don't care if you don't think the deadline is important. For reasons you may not know about, it's important to the client. Do whatever it takes, but hit it. Trust me—your value to the employer or client will rise enormously, and that's always worth it.

Be the person who everyone knows will always hit the deadline, and you'll be working for life.

35

CHAPTER 2

EXPECTATIONS MATTER

START DEALING WITH THEM

*Exceed your customer's expectations. If you
do, they'll come back over and over. Give them
what they want—and a little more.*

—Sam Walton, founder of Walmart

Whenever you develop great ideas or produce creative projects,
it should go without saying that you have to consider client,
audience, or customer expectations. I was reminded of that
recently when the latest statistics came out about airline versus automobile deaths in America. Far more people die of car crashes every year,

but generally, the public is much more terrified of dying in an airplane accident. The expectation of the public totally overwhelms reality. As a result, the government has to take that erroneous public perception into consideration in its legislation, rules, and policies for both industries.

As a leader of creative people, it's critical to understand your client, audience, or customer's expectations. Remember—even when those expectations may not be grounded in reality, you can't ignore them. As the saying goes, right or wrong, *perception is reality*.

You will always fail if you disregard expectations.

That doesn't mean you can't deliver *beyond* what they expect. We talk about "exceeding" expectations, but to accomplish that, you have to know those expectations at the start. That's why one of the most difficult challenges I personally face with clients is *managing their expectations*. It happens in a million ways. Sometimes they don't have all the information; other times their past experience colors the relationship, or they simply don't have the experience to evaluate success. Whatever the cause, it's up to you to manage the outcome.

Why?

Because whether you're a client-driven business or dealing with a boss or supervisor, your success depends on meeting—and exceeding—their expectations. To make that happen, here are a few suggestions:

1) **Be direct.** Most client, boss, or supervisor relationships fail simply because there are misunderstandings. Ask questions. Be specific. Don't leave the meeting without knowing exactly what they want you to accomplish. We'll talk about "clarity" later in the book because it's critical to understanding expectations.

   I once knew a TV commercial producer who was always afraid to be frank with clients and ask the right questions upfront. In every case, it resulted in massive reedits at best or projects being pulled at worst. Be gracious, but be direct. Never be afraid to ask that one question that's bugging the heck out of you.

2) **Be honest.** Let them know what you can and can't do. Don't be embarrassed to tell them your weakness. I used to work with a guy who was ashamed to tell the boss that he couldn't deliver on certain things. As a result, he kept missing deadlines which cost us dearly. The boss or client would much rather know your strengths and weaknesses upfront than to find out the night before the deadline.

Many leadership coaches and teachers tell leaders to work on their weaknesses, and that's why so many aren't honest with clients, bosses, or customers. They're working on those weaknesses, so they don't bring it up. I'm the opposite. Rather than wasting time working on my weakest areas, I choose to spend that time becoming better at my strengths. My strengths are what I'm selling.

3) **Don't assume.** Most of the times I've gotten into trouble have been when I "assumed" the client understood what I meant. I wasn't clear and specific. I didn't check. That always gets you into trouble.

4) **Over deliver.** Your boss or client thinks you're an expert in your field, so prove it. If they find mistakes in your work, they'll start wondering why they hired you in the first place. Set a high bar, and always deliver. If possible, deliver early. It will make a huge impression.

5) **Give them options.** Sometimes, things don't work out like either of you expect. In those cases, tell them you understand the situation, and provide them options. Let them know you care about their project more than they do. That attitude alone can win you a client for life.

Facts are one thing, but *expectations* are another. Don't think both automatically match, and always be concerned about perceptions and expectations. When you don't manage them, disaster can easily happen. As I mentioned earlier, for me, it's the most challenging aspect of working with clients, but getting on the same page with what they expect and what you deliver is critical.

It's just as important when it comes to the day-to-day expectations of co-workers, family, and friends. For instance, time and time again, people want to meet with me but not tell me in advance what it's about. In a similar way, people invite co-workers to meetings without an agenda. Others ask for help but don't tell you exactly what's expected. Still others drop in uninvited with no advance warning.

In the case of meetings, knowing your expectations allows me to plan, so our time together can be more productive. Even in friendship or marriage, it's a simple courtesy to let the other person know when you expect to arrive, what you plan to do, or what you want to discuss.

Don't confuse clear expectations with trust.

We erroneously believe that because we're friends or co-workers, I don't have to tell you why we need to meet or why I'm coming over. But not only is it wrong, it's disrespectful and rude. Setting expectations has nothing to do with friendship or trust. It's simply common courtesy to help people plan. It tells them that you value their time.

CHAPTER 3

THE TRUTH ABOUT THE *EUREKA* MOMENT

Ideas don't magically appear in a genius's head from nowhere. They always build on what came before.

—R. Keith Sawyer, researcher

A frustrating myth about creativity is the "eureka" or "aha" moment—the popular concept that brilliant ideas just pop into our heads out of nowhere. It's persistent because, on the surface, it does seem to be what's happening. Think about your own experience—how often has a world-changing idea just seemed to appear out of nowhere? It might have been on a walk, in the shower, or driving.

But on closer inspection, that "aha" moment was simply the culmination of hours and hours of work putting all the pieces together. In a special edition of *Time* magazine, researcher R. Keith Sawyer, author of the book *Explaining Creativity: The Science of Human Innovation*, put it this way:

> *Many people believe creativity comes in a sudden moment of insight and that this "magical" burst of an idea is a different mental process from our everyday thinking. But extensive research has shown that when you're creative, your brain is using the same mental building blocks you use every day like when you figure out a way around a traffic jam.*

In other words, it's about the *process*, not the *moment*. I may spend hours and hours writing a script and then hit a wall. So I take a walk, go to the beach, or take a drive. During that time, if the answer comes, it's not "out of the blue," it's simply the logical conclusion of my mind working out the problem subconsciously. Sawyer described the team trying to fix the Hubble telescope as an example:

> *In 1990 a team of NASA scientists was trying to fix the distorted lenses in the Hubble telescope, which was already in orbit. An expert in optics suggested that tiny inversely distorted mirrors could correct the images, but nobody could figure out how to fit them into the hard-to-reach space inside. Then engineer Jim Crocker, taking a shower in a German hotel, noticed the European-style shower head mounted on adjustable rods. He realized the Hubble's little mirrors could be extended into the telescope by mounting them on similar folding arms. And this flash was the key to fixing the problem.*

That "flash" wasn't an idea handed to him from the idea gods; it was the result of a long period of intense work on the problem. That moment in the shower, when Jim Crocker saw the adjustable shower rod, it all just came together.

> *It was in that room too that I learned not to think about anything that I was writing from the time I stopped writing until I started again the next day. That way my subconscious would be working on it and at the same time I would be listening to other people and noticing everything.*
> —ERNEST HEMINGWAY, NOVELIST

This is important to understand because so many people assume the idea will come without doing the hard work first. Without that serious work, the building blocks of the idea can't form because they have no foundation. Creative ideas aren't random explosions, they're the result of a process of trying and failing and trying and failing again. Only then can the connections happen that change the world.

MAKE EUREKA MOMENTS WORK FOR YOU

Now that you understand where that eureka moment comes from, the secret is positioning yourself to have more of those moments. Here are five keys that will help:

1) **Notice everything.** I'll never forget driving outside Dallas with a friend a number of years ago. I noticed a strange light sculpture miles away in the distance and mentioned it. My friend said, "One thing about you is that you notice things nobody else sees." For creative breakthroughs, open your eyes and start seeing the world that no one else notices.

2) **Write it down.** One group of researchers studied people conducting hiring interviews. In the cases where the interviewers took notes about their conversations with each of the candidates, they were able to recall about 23 percent more information than people who didn't take notes. We'll talk about this more, but for

right now, remember that there's something about the physical act of writing things down that helps lock it into our memory.

3) **Ask questions.** There's a Chinese proverb that says, "He who asks a question is a fool for five minutes. He who does not ask a question is a fool forever."

4) **Do nothing.** Sometimes our "busyness" clutters our lives and fogs our brain. Don't forget to take the time to pause and reflect. Over my career, most of my best ideas came to me when I was bored out of my mind. There's just something about quiet reflection that makes remarkable mental connections happen.

5) **Read more.** I'm amazed how often I sit next to people on plane flights that either just sit there or play video games. Nothing wrong with video games, but sometimes you need to feed the creative engine inside. What are you reading? Is it a celebrity magazine or something that can impact your life and career? And don't shy away from longer books. Sometimes it takes time to develop a powerful idea, and if all you're reading is short posts or magazine articles, you'll miss much of the richness of deep thinking.

Breakthrough ideas and eureka moments seem like they "just happen," but the truth is, people who do have them have created the atmosphere where they happen more often.

43

CHAPTER 4

WHY PASSION ISN'T ENOUGH

There's a dangerously limiting idea at the heart of everything we believe about success and life in general and that is that you have one singular passion and it's your job to find it, pursue it to the exclusion of everything else and if you do, everything will fall into place. And if you don't, you've failed.

—Terri Trespicio, brand advisor

We've all heard so much about "passion" when it comes to our career or calling. People want to be passionate about their work, so they search for a career they can feel passionate about. There are millions of inspiring quotes about passion and a library of books written on the subject. However, for me, passion falls in the area of "feelings," and if you've been on this earth very long, you know that we simply can't control—*or even trust*—our feelings. Those whose creative careers are driven by passion can experience very high peaks, but they also have to trudge through dry spells that can last a long time.

The truth is, passion is transitory, temporary, and often shallow. It has too many ups and downs. When you're in the zone, passion is great, but when it comes to a long career or projects that must be regularly delivered on budget and on time, it simply won't get you very far.

So what do I recommend?

Hunger.

> ### When it comes to your career or calling, my advice is this: Your "passion" is what you want. Your "hunger" is what you can't live without.

Passion too often gets confused with what people enjoy, what they find easy to do, or what seems trendy at the moment. That's a big reason I get so many film scripts mailed to me with cover letters telling me how passionate the writer is about writing. But the problem is, you don't need to read many pages before you realize they're simply terrible writers. That's why I encourage you, instead, to search for your deep hunger.

If passion is something you can live without, hunger is what you need to survive. That's why you need to spend less time finding your passion and more time discovering what you are actually *wired* to do.

For instance, if writing is your passion, you may enjoy it, but when that passion subsides, you'll move on to something else. But if writing is a hunger, then you can't live without it. If you're a writer, then you'll write every day, you'll write no matter how many critics, and you'll write without getting paid.

You write because you can't not write.

That idea is why I wrote the book *One Big Thing: Discovering What You Were Born to Do*. The bottom line is that in today's demanding, hyper-competitive world, hunger is fierce and unrelenting, and will eat passion for lunch.

> *Creativity is a highfalutin word for the work*
> *I have to do between now and Tuesday.*
> —RAY KROC, FOUNDER OF McDONALD'S

When I teach filmmakers or speak at conferences, I invariably get one person who tells me that their passion is to produce a movie and wants my advice. Great. I couldn't be more thrilled. But then I ask the big question:

"What training do you have?"

The answer? "None."

So I follow up:

"Are you going to attend film school?"

"No—that takes too long."

"Are you planning to move to Hollywood or New York?"

"I don't want to move."

"Are you working on an internship or working as a filmmaker's assistant?"

"No. I need a paid job."

"Have you taken an online course?"

"No, they're too expensive."

"Have you written, or have you acquired a script?"

"No."

"Do you have a plan?"

"No. That's why I need your advice."

At that point, I get exasperated, wish them well, and walk away. To show you how frustrated it makes me, let me frame it a different way:

"Phil, I really feel passionate about becoming a brain surgeon."

"Great, what training do you have?"

"None. I've been selling insurance, but I really feel that my purpose is to be a brain surgeon, and I'm very passionate about it. However, the thing is, I don't have time to go to medical school and then do that whole residency thing. It would take too long, and it's really expensive."

"So what's your plan?"

"I don't know. That's why I need your advice."

Get it? So if you're one of those people who are convinced that you have a rare gift, remarkable talent, the greatest idea ever, or you're on a mission from God, here's my answer:

To be a success in today's world, you need to be disciplined, ready to work, and make more than a few sacrifices. Honestly, I don't have any advice for someone who believes they're a rare gem who will break through without any obstacles. It doesn't happen to brain surgeons, and it won't happen to you.

Now, let's get on with it.

WHEN I CAME TO THE END OF PASSION

I'm going to open up a bit here and tell a story I've rarely told anyone. When I started in this business, my passion was to be a film director. I studied it in college, was one of the most driven students in film school, and was always working for a media company during school—as an assistant, gofer, pushing camera dollies, driving, whatever it took. In fact, I would often get into trouble on the set because, instead of focusing on my job, I was watching the director and making mental notes about how he or she worked. I studied it day and night, and today, my personal library is filled with books on film directing and biographies of the most talented and famous film and theater directors in history.

Over the years, I've directed programming in nearly seventy countries around the world, including the widest variety of documentaries, TV programs, commercials, sports, and concert events you could imagine. I've directed pretty much anything you can think of that can be shot with a camera.

Which means, early on, I would direct anything that walked. I did my share of hot tub commercials, infomercials for "miracle" products, TV evangelists, industrial films, and I even attempted a powerful and moving promotional film on a company that manufactured sewer pipes. (For the record, the client loved it.)

I eventually became a partner in an A-list commercial production company with a team of directors that filmed TV spots all over the world, including Super Bowl commercials.

It was in Vancouver, Canada, that I hit my ceiling as a director.

We had been approached by a Japanese advertising agency (the largest in the world at the time) to produce a short film for one of their clients. It was a fantastic project because it had a great budget, but even better—it wasn't about selling the product, it was about inspiring the audience, and their plan was to show the film in an international campaign to promote the company.

So we decided to shoot in Vancouver, planned the production, cast the actors, and started filming. We had a terrific crew and everything was going well until about the mid-point of the project. That's when I realized that I was ultimately unable to get exactly what I needed from the actors.

They were very talented actors, but we reached a point where suddenly my ability to communicate what I wanted wasn't working.

But wait a minute—I've directed projects all over the world, in every situation you can imagine, and have plenty of awards to prove it. What's going on here?

I was baffled.

Over the course of the shooting, I would go back to my hotel room and reflect on my frustration. And toward the end of the project, I came to a painful and difficult revelation:

I didn't have the directing gifts and talent to go where I wanted to go with my career.

The problem was that I *was* very good. After all, I had a wall full of awards, I had been tapped by a major advertising agency for the project, and I had a very long list of previously successful projects. To most of my family, friends, and associates, I was doing great.

But inside and unknown to anyone else, I knew the place I wanted to go with my career, and because of that target, I also realized that I would come up short. I realized that my passion had only taken me part of the journey.

The rest of the trip would need to be on the back of my talent.

Inside, I knew I'd reached the limit of my directing skill, and it was time to take a deeper dive and discover what I was actually *wired* to do. After a great deal more painful reflection, I realized that I had written almost everything I had ever directed, perhaps more than that because of budget reasons early in my career, I had produced or co-produced nearly every project as well.

By that time, I wasn't just writing TV programs and commercials, I was writing books and doing creative consulting for major organizations. At the same time, I had produced global satellite events for television and even stepped up to produce a feature film when the original producers had dropped the ball.

When I really thought about it, writing and producing came relatively easy for me—so easy I hadn't even noticed—*because I was wired for it.* Today, on network television, there's a title called "showrunner" which denotes the person who is the ultimate leader of an episodic TV or streaming series. In most cases, they have written the pilot episode, continue to write most others, and make the final decisions when it comes to producing the series.

Back when I started in the business, I'd never heard of that title, but if I had, that's the role I would have pursued.

IT GETS WORSE.

I started to wonder how many years (even decades) I lost pursuing my *passion* instead of focusing on what I was actually *gifted to accomplish*. Ultimately, my "wiring" wasn't about directing as much as coming up with the original concept, writing it, and supervising the production of the show. What if I'd pursued that from the start of my career with the same enthusiasm I'd put into directing?

Where might I be today?

And here's the thing: once you discover that thing you're wired to do, you'll get pretty passionate about it. In my case, when I discovered my real gifts, my career turned a major corner. I started writing with more enthusiasm, built a great production team around me, and even my energy level increased. We started attracting bigger clients and projects.

That's why it's so important as we begin this journey that you take a hard look at why you're here and what you're wired to do with your life.

IDEAS ON A DEADLINE

If you saw Ken Burns's remarkable documentary series on the Civil War, then you'll remember author Shelby Foote, one of the most respected writers on that era. In writing about passion and inspiration, here's his take:

> *I'm privately convinced that most of the really bad writing the world has ever seen has been done under the influence of what's called inspiration. Writing is very hard work and knowing what you're doing the whole time.*

Stop pursuing passion, and let it come to you. Focus less on what you're passionate about right now, and take the deep dive toward discovering your real gifts and talents. Once that happens, I can guarantee your passion will show up right on time. *Because nothing inspires passion like discovering what you were created to accomplish.*

51

PART 2
THE MOTIVATION
THE ART OF THE CREATIVE ATTITUDE

My chief work in advertising has been meeting emergencies. Nobody ever called me in when the skies were bright, and the seas were calm. Nearly every client quit me when he got into smooth waters.

—Claude Hopkins, advertising legend

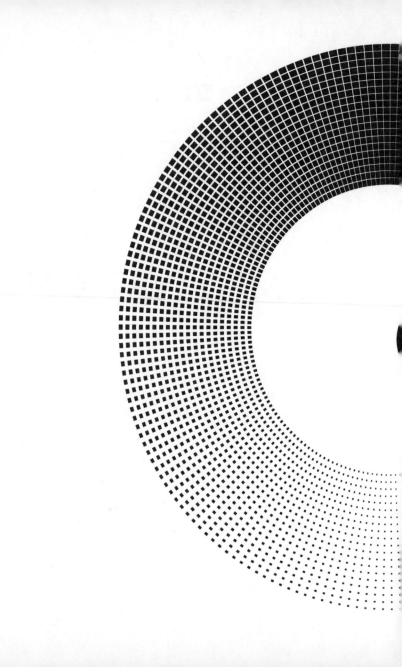

53

CHAPTER 5

START BY SAYING "NO"

*A dominant myth in almost every workplace
is that if you say no, you will be shot.*

—Peter Block, *The Answer to How is Yes*

At this point, it's time to start thinking about the motivation it takes to be a professional creative—especially when the clock is ticking. And one of the first lessons we have to learn about creating great ideas on a deadline is to free up our limited creative time by saying no to other demands. We live in a world today where we've all been drafted into the productivity cult. And the truth is, there's something to be said for being organized. While I'm not a fanatic, I do believe that if you're spending all your time searching for documents, clippings, books, files, or other materials, that simply takes away from creative time.

But there are also those who are obsessed with simply *being busy*. I noticed it long before the computer age. Early in my career, I worked with a manager who spent the first hour or two of his morning just getting his to-do list down. It was a work of art—nice lines, boxes to be checked, very organized. He constantly told everyone how "busy" he was but the only problem? He rarely ever accomplished anything significant. He was simply too busy keeping his to-do list up to date.

But there's something even more sinister about the productivity movement, and that's the attitude that if you're not busy, you're not accomplishing anything. As a result, I have friends who don't talk about *accomplishment*; they constantly talk about *being busy*.

"Hi, what are you doing?"

"Oh, you know—just staying busy!"

"Did you have a good day today?"

"No—I have so much to do; I barely scratched the surface."

Writer Tim Kreider put it this way:

> Busyness serves as a kind of existential reassurance, a hedge against emptiness; obviously your life cannot possibly be silly or trivial or meaningless if you are so busy. . . . I can't help but wonder whether all this histrionic exhaustion isn't a way of covering up the fact that most of what we do doesn't matter.

Maybe it's time we worried less about being *busy* and more about being *significant*. Then again, significance takes deep thought, focus, and reflection. And in today's distracted world, it's probably easier just to be busy.

Do you return every phone call, text message, and e-mail? I'm not sure about you, but I don't. I don't believe we're obligated to respond to everyone who calls, texts, e-mails, or otherwise reaches out. Certainly we want to be gracious, and we never want to be rude or condescending.

However, if you're going to accomplish something that matters with your life, you simply can't say YES to everyone.

Think about it. If I called the chairman of a Hollywood studio at random right now, what are the odds that he'd actually respond? Pretty low. They have much bigger fish to fry.

But today, people feel powerfully compelled to answer the phone, even in the most awkward situations. I was talking to a friend the other day, and his cell phone rang. He actually interrupted our face-to-face conversation to answer the phone and say, "I'm sorry; I can't talk right now. Can I call you back in an hour?"

Wait—isn't that what voicemail is for?

It's been said that if you spend all day responding to phone calls and e-mail, then you're spending your day responding to other people's priorities.

It's especially difficult for creative professionals because we're service providers. We work with clients or bosses, so, within reason, we always want to be available. But even our clients know we're not helping them by constantly being in response mode. They also want us working on what we do best because that's what moves the needle.

The point is, to increase the quality of your ideas when the clock is ticking—*start valuing your time*. Start focusing on your work. If you can gang up your return calls, texts, and e-mails later in the day, fine—but even then, prioritize whom you respond to and why. For now, consider yourself free from the overwhelming need to respond to everyone. It's not only unnecessary, but if you don't prioritize, it will eventually derail your creative career.

> *The difference between successful people and*
> *really successful people is that really successful*
> *people say "no" most of the time.*
> —WARREN BUFFETT, INVESTOR

And there's a far bigger perspective than not answering every phone call, text, or e-mail. When it comes to being creative, if we want to make that deadline or accomplish our goal, we will have to say no to other people, projects, and choices. The late co-founder and former CEO of Apple, Steve Jobs, put it this way:

> *People think focus means saying yes to the thing you've got to*
> *focus on. But that's not what it means at all. It means saying no*
> *to the hundred other good ideas that there are. You have to pick*
> *carefully. I'm actually as proud of the things we haven't done as*
> *the things I have done. Innovation is saying no to 1,000 things.*

Are you focusing on the things you should be focusing on and saying no to everything else? Are you saying no to the harsh critics and destructive people who shouldn't be in your life or business? Are you saying no to the million distractions that surround us every day? Are you saying no to the *good* opportunities to make the time for *great* opportunities?

When was the last time you said no at all?

> **It is extremely important to be able to make negative**
> **assertions. We must be able to say what is "not me" in**
> **order to have a "me." What we like has no meaning**
> **unless we know what we don't like. Our yes has no**
> **meaning if we never say no. My chosen profession**
> **has no passion if "just anyone would do."**

> **Our opinions and thoughts mean very little**
> **if there is nothing we disagree with.**[4]
> —DR. HENRY CLOUD, *CHANGES THAT HEAL*

---

4 Henry Cloud, *Changes That Heal: The Four Shifts That Make Everything Better . . . and That Anyone Can Do* (Grand Rapids: Zondervan, 1992).

Whenever I speak on this subject, I always get a positive response from the audience. We all know that we get pulled into more things than we can possibly do, and most of the time, it's because we just can't say no. And many of us feel the obligation to be kind, so we really hate to turn people down. But the bottom line is that until we start saying no to some things, we'll never have time to pursue the really important things.

I would encourage you to stop and reflect on this for a moment because most creative people are also very nice people. I know because I'm a people pleaser. We want to be helpful because it's our nature. As a result, we constantly allow ourselves to be interrupted and often allow ourselves to be taken advantage of even when we know better.

Ultimately, it creates roadblocks on the journey to delivering our ideas on schedule. Many reading this will need some practice in the art of turning people down. We never want to be a jerk about it, so if you suffer from the inability to turn people down, here are some good examples of how to respond when you're asked to do something you really don't want or need to do:

1) **"Let me check my schedule first."**

   This implies you have other things on your plate (which you do) and keeps you from answering on the spot. Take some time, check your calendar and to-do list, think about your priorities, and get back to them later. In many cases, by that time, they'll have found someone else.

2) **"That's not a priority for me right now."**

   Yes, you do have other priorities, and they matter. It's always good to remind people of what you're focused on in your life and career, and in many cases, what they want you to do isn't on that list.

3) **"I'd love to, but I'm in the middle of another project. Maybe next time."**

   This positions you as being open to the possibility, but you just can't do it now. End of story.

4) **"I'm (insert traveling, writing, closing a deal, designing, prepping a project, facing a deadline, etc.) right now, and it will be awhile before I have enough time to make that happen."**

This is very true for most of us. We're working, and it's a real imposition to ask us to read a script, evaluate a project, or let them pick our brain.

Notice that none of these answers are meant to offend. They all tell the truth about your situation and allow you the breathing room to focus on the projects you feel matter. Certainly, we want to be gracious and help when we can, but in those moments when someone crosses the line, these are good responses.

And don't lie because that's not the answer either. We need to be truthful, but when you look at the list above, you can see plenty of perfectly honest and appropriate ways to say no.

In the final analysis, when the clock is ticking, and we're working on a creative idea or project, you need to clear a path to the goal, and nothing will clear that path more effectively than saying no to anything else that fights for your attention. Just try it, and the more you do it, the more comfortable it will become.

The real truth here is that we need to stop automatically responding to what other people think is urgent and start focusing on what we think is important.

59

CHAPTER 6

LEARN TO FORGET WHAT YOU KNOW

You are lost the minute you know what the result will be.

—Juan Gris, artist

Back when our granddaughter Kennady was a year old, she'd had very little time to learn how things worked. As a result, the first few times I gave her a book, she had no idea what "reading" was, so she walked on it, set it up like an A-frame house, or used it for a plate. Back then, it was that way with everything. Since she didn't know the way things were "supposed" to be used, she just made it up, and she came up with some pretty remarkable uses for things like spoons, a flute, a ball—not to mention food.

One day while watching her, it hit me: people who are less creative always default to what we're *supposed* to do with things.

People who are more creative have the ability to set those expectations aside and approach it ... with no preconceived ideas.

Here's an old exercise to find out who's creative on your team: Take something everyone knows—like a hammer, an umbrella, or a stool. Ask each person to come up with something completely different—and legitimate—that item could be used for.

You'll find out pretty quickly, who's bound by what they know, and who's able to set that knowledge aside and start seeing new possibilities.

Why does it matter? Because during your career, you'll be asked to come up with new ideas for things everyone already knows. Perhaps a new way to structure your team, a new approach to marketing, a different way to look at a client's problem, or a different use for a product. Remember that pretty much everyone looked at mobile phones the same way until Apple's creative team came along and set aside that perspective and viewed it from a completely different angle.

The idea for Henry Ford's assembly line for building automobiles came from seeing how a slaughterhouse worked. The dead animal was hung from a conveyor belt, and instead of the employees moving, the meat traveled from employee to employee since each was responsible for a different act: carving, butchering, or packaging. Applying the same concept to the manufacture of automobiles transformed the car industry.

Early in my career, I was hired to create an advertising campaign for an obscure company that manufactured drainage pipes. The founder of the company had been hired years before by a number of cities and towns to replace cracked, aging, and sometimes collapsed underground concrete pipes. The problem was that it required the expensive and time-consuming process of digging up miles of heavy concrete pipe, replacing it, and then covering it back up.

But he looked at the problem differently. He started manufacturing *plastic* pipe that was just a tiny bit smaller than the concrete pipes. Then he could start at one end, pull the new plastic pipe through the existing concrete sections so it could be replaced with no digging far more quickly and at a lower cost. Plus, the new plastic pipe wasn't nearly as susceptible to cracking from weather and would last far longer.

Everyone else looked at how it was always done, but he saw something completely new.

The business idea of "best practices" is a great concept for doing the same thing better. But we need to look *beyond* best practices to what *new* ideas could come from an existing product, service, or concept.

Whatever the task, you'll be more successful if you can sometimes set aside your "knowledge" and look at it like my granddaughter.

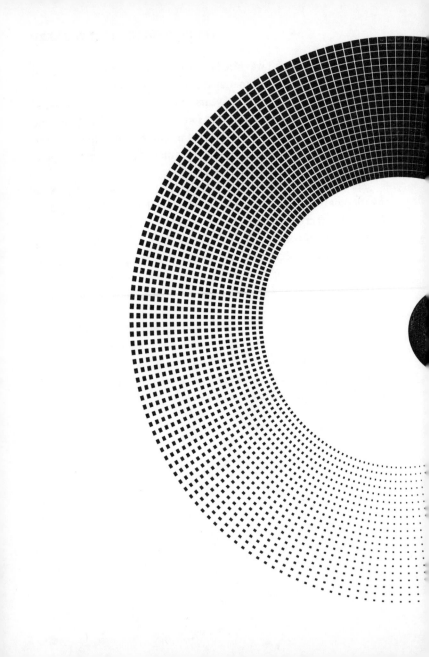

CHAPTER 7

PUSH THE BOUNDARIES AND BUILD CREATIVE CONFIDENCE

I'd rather apologize than be so timid as to never try to do anything smart or brave.

—Lee Clow, advertising creative director

To access creative ideas when you need them requires the ironic combination of humility and confidence. Humility matters because, in my experience, one of the greatest threats to creative professionals is pride. It's why so few artists and creatives can survive a long career. At some point, they start taking creativity for granted, and like a romantic relationship, things start to sour.

A good dose of humility keeps you hungry for more, keeps you learning, and keeps you growing. I've noticed that after periods when I won awards or received positive media coverage I was most likely to get stuck in my thinking. When we get noticed for our work, we tend to remember that acclaim and keep doing what got us all that attention. The problem is the world changes, and if we don't change with it, we'll simply be left behind.

Pride was probably the original sin which makes it so hard to overcome. Someone told me early in my career to be nice to everyone I meet on the way up because I'll see them again on my way back down. Staying vigilant as we grow in our talent is critical to our growth as a professional.

On the other hand, without *confidence*, we won't get very far—but confidence is hard to build in the creative world. You can't imagine the number of leaders I find who have lost that confidence. They've stopped asking questions about their purpose, their process, or their results. "We've always done it that way," has become a mantra for far too many leaders who have stopped questioning.

Let's face it—creativity is hard.

Coming up with breakthrough ideas is difficult business at best, and at worst, it can make you physically sick. Novelist Lawrence Durrell described the frustrations of all creative work when he said:

> I have discovered quite recently that the characteristic Freudian resistance to confessions of any sort, which are very well represented in all the writing blocks one goes through—the dizzy

fits, the nauseas, and so forth, which almost every writer has recorded—are a standard pattern for all kinds of creative things.

INSTITUTIONAL THINKING

That difficulty is a big reason many people become *institutionalized* when it comes to creative thinking. They play it safe, stop taking risks, and look for the easy way out. The truth is, nobody starts out to be average. So the question becomes, how did they get that way?

I'm reminded of the quote by the prison inmate "Red" played by Morgan Freeman when he described his older friend "Brooks" in the movie *The Shawshank Redemption*. When asked why Brooks didn't want to leave the prison—even though his sentence was served—Red replied: "First you hate the walls, then you get used to them, then you depend on them."

At first, creative people hate average. They push the boundaries and really want to make a difference in the culture. They're willing to put in the hours, take the criticism, and fight for what they believe in.

But after a while, they get tired of the long hours, the critical clients, investors, or donors who don't get it. They ease up, thinking that it just takes time, so why push it? After all, those who are pushing back are the big clients or supporters, so let's not upset them. We'll give it some time, and people will change. It's perfectly understandable.

But after a few more years, they get used to the regular hours, the support of influential people, and never having to defend their ideas. After all, it's easier; why rock the boat? So they leave the freelance life and take a full-time job. Or they stop pushing their team. CEOs enjoy the support of the board.

Before long, they depend on the walls. If they're honest, they'll admit that they look fondly back on the old creative days but realize now it was just a youthful phase. Now, they understand that creativity, business, or nonprofit work is serious. So they work within the system.

They lie to themselves.

Fortunately, some realize their mistake and break out of the walls. It's tough—very tough. But for most, living inside the walls works. It's easier to go unchallenged, have a nice office, and keep the respect of those who love the way things have always been done.

So the question is—where are you right now? At what point did you get bought off with a raise? At what point did you give up? And perhaps, more importantly, what are you willing to do to break out of those walls?

THE BIAS BATTLE

It took me many years to develop a thick skin, and over that time, my confidence was easily damaged. For much of my career, the "creative types" were never taken seriously when it came to an organization's leadership. While we were valued, we weren't considered responsible enough to assume a leadership role, and over and over again, those roles went to less talented non-creative members of the team.

Early in my career, I worked for a very large media organization. Although I was the person in the media department the organization's founder spent the most time with, and I was the person who made most of the creative decisions surrounding our programming—and perhaps, most importantly—I was the person the employees looked to when a creative decision had to be made, I was continually passed over to be head of the department.

Time and time again, the choice went to someone far less creative—sometimes, with little or no media experience at all. So even back in my twenties, I understood that management often has a leadership bias against creatives.

Perhaps you've discovered that in your career.

Now, research studies are proving what I learned way back then: Creative expression often hurts your chances of a leadership position. It's wrong, but sadly, it's true in many organizations. So what can you do?

GROW YOUR CONFIDENCE.

Become the expert in your field. Read, study, be proactive in your career. When armed with evidence of your expertise, bias tends to weaken. Bias is most powerful when there is nothing else concrete to go on—that's when our brains (unconsciously) fill in the blanks.

Don't get stuck focusing on your past experience. Focus on your leadership potential—the kind of creative leader you see yourself becoming. Studies show that interviewers are drawn to candidates described as having potential (often more than actual achievement). They'll spend more time thinking about you, and that extra thinking results in more accuracy and less bias.

Tackle the bias head-on. Acknowledge that creative types aren't often chosen for leadership positions, while arguing (nicely) that your ability to offer fresh and innovative solutions to problems is essential to effective leadership rather than at odds with it.

> *Like a muscle, your creative abilities will*
> *grow and strengthen with practice.[5]*
> —TOM KELLEY, *CREATIVE CONFIDENCE: UNLEASHING*
> *THE CREATIVE POTENTIAL WITHIN US ALL*

The truth is the world needs more creative thinking in every area of life. We need more creative teachers, real estate agents, sales professionals, pastors, insurance executives, and office managers. We need more creative parents and grandparents. We need more creative minds in government, business, science, and the nonprofit world. In short, everyone could stand a creative overhaul—understanding a new way to do things that brings better results.

But that road isn't easy. A single piano lesson doesn't qualify a pianist for an international concert career. It takes years and years of practice and rehearsal before careers are launched, and it's not that different in

---

5   Tom Kelley and David Kelley, *Creative Confidence: Unleashing the Creative Potential within Us All* (London: William Collins, 2015).

creative fields. I look back with embarrassment on all the wacky product infomercials, hot tub commercials, and other crazy stuff I wrote and produced early in my career. But honestly, they taught me the copywriting rules of the road. I didn't have any mentors back in those days, so I had to beat my head against the brick wall of experience. Dealing with a few insane clients, having a limited budget, working with cheap equipment—all were the training ground for my understanding how television generated a response from the audience.

But my secret was starting small.

> *I purposely look for crackpot and harebrained ideas to see if any of them shows potential. When I talk to a vendor about my application and he says, "Oh, yeah, you use the material like this," I usually lose interest. There is no use in trying an approach that everyone else knows about. But if a vendor tells me, "Oh, no, nobody does it that way," I get all excited since I know I've hit pay dirt.*
> —MARK HUBER, RESEARCH AND DEVELOPMENT,
> WALT DISNEY IMAGINEERING

To start building your creative confidence, start asking questions. Don't be afraid to try the harebrained ideas. You don't have to be the obstinate employee on the team or the grumpy friend, but you *can* start looking at other ways to make things happen.

Perhaps it's because I've been doing it so long, I can't stand to drive the same routes to work, the airport, the grocery store, or a friend's house. It drives my family crazy, but I want to see what would happen if we took another path.

Little ideas like that can start you on the road to looking at life in different ways.

CHAPTER 8

IT'S TIME TO EMBRACE THE FEAR

Everything you want is on the other side of fear.

—Jack Canfield, motivational speaker and entrepreneur

Millions of people spend an enormous amount of time, effort, and money trying to live without fear or anxiety. We read books about being brave, take classes in gaining confidence, and spend tons of money on inspirational books and courses. That's not necessarily a bad thing—except for the fact that fear is one of the most powerful motivators on the planet. Fear of danger kept early human beings alive. Fear of war kept leaders working at diplomacy. Fear of poverty kept our parents and grandparents working hard. And today, while many of the things we fear may have changed, the emotion is just as powerful—and important.

I see too many creative leaders living in denial because they refuse to acknowledge the fear that their business or nonprofit is failing. I see others with no self-awareness because to face their shortcomings would create too much fear.

> **That ability to know ourselves immediately puts us ahead of the pack because in today's professional world, self-awareness is a rare commodity.**

In her book *Insight: Why We're Not as Self-Aware as We Think, and How Seeing Ourselves Clearly Helps Us Succeed*, organizational psychologist Tasha Eurich says:

> There is strong scientific evidence that people who know themselves and how others see them are happier. They make smarter decisions. They have better personal and professional relationships. They raise more mature children. They're smarter, superior students who choose better careers. They're more creative, more confident, and better communicators. They're less aggressive and less likely to lie, cheat, and steal. They're better performers at work who get more promotions. They're more effective leaders with more enthusiastic employees. They even lead more profitable companies.[6]

Her research confirms what most of us have experienced, that the *least* competent people are usually the *most* confident in their abilities.

---

6   Tasha Eurich, *Insight: Why We're Not as Self-Aware as We Think, and How Seeing Ourselves Clearly Helps Us Succeed at Work and in Life* (London: Crown Business, 2017).

But a realistic and healthy self-image is the foundation for a long, creative career.

Certainly there are overblown fears. When what I would call a "healthy" fear is replaced by an unfounded or out-of-proportion fear, that's a bigger issue that needs to be dealt with in other ways.

But for most creative professionals, most of the time, we need to embrace it. Look your fear in the face. Understand where it comes from. Your fear is the canary in the coal mine. It could be the early warning sign that something needs to change.

That uncomfortable feeling in your gut when you do certain things or make certain decisions shouldn't be ignored, it should be welcomed.

And here's the important point: Fear becomes your friend, not when it's gone, but when it's overcome. When you're self-aware, you recognize the fear for what it really is and act on it in a way that solves the problem. Your response to the fear is to fix the reason it's there.

Stop ignoring it, worrying about it, or denying it, and start responding to it.

We all know the immediate fear that engulfs us when we're given a creative assignment with a looming deadline. It can make your heart race, you get a bit light-headed, and you're flooded with thoughts of failure.

I certainly felt all those emotions sitting alone in that conference room outside of Marty Krofft's office in Hollywood, and I've felt it many times since. But fear can work *against* you or work *for* you. It's all in how you react.

For some creative people, fear and anxiety can be crippling, and I don't want to deny that fact. Fear and anxiety come in all shapes, sizes, and attacks in different ways. But from a career perspective, if you want to turn the tables and take charge of your fear, here's my advice:

1) **Acknowledge the fear.**

   Fear starts losing its power the minute we acknowledge it and make it public. Stop trying to hide it (everyone knows about it anyway). Get it out there. Let everyone know it's a challenge for you, but you're going to stand up to it.

2) **Do something about it.**

   Making it public does something great—it forces you to act. Otherwise, you'll be humiliated. Share it with a friend, take a class, talk to a counselor, pray about it, find a mentor—whatever it takes to figure this out and move forward. Fear does the most damage when people keep it bottled up inside.

3) **Celebrate small victories.**

   You don't have to overcome your fear instantly. Take small steps and celebrate each one. Let people know your progress, so they can celebrate with you. That alone is a huge momentum builder.

4) **Beat the fear with knowledge.**

   A friend of mine was afraid of water, so she took a swim class and immediately took the next step of being certified for scuba diving! All that classroom time built up her confidence, and eventually, she loved taking her first dive. Another was afraid of heights, so he took skydiving lessons. Remember, they don't toss you out of a plane on the first day. You spend time learning in the classroom, and that knowledge gave him enormous motivation and confidence. Education is a powerful tool for overcoming your fear.

5) **Finally, be realistic.**

   The truth is, your fear of public speaking is nothing compared to people's desire to hear what you have to say. The reward is so much greater than the struggle. Talk to other people. Listen to them, and believe them. Most fears are exaggerated, and although that doesn't lessen their power, seeing the world realistically makes a big difference.

Don't run from your fear. Humbly acknowledge it, realize that you need to conquer it next time, and then make the effort to move forward. Otherwise, you can be trapped in fear for the rest of your life.

THE EVIL OF COMPARISON

One of the greatest causes of fear in creative people is *comparison*. Particularly in the age of social media, we human beings tend to constantly compare ourselves against our friends, rivals, coworkers, competitors, or enemies. But out of context, comparison will always destroy.

I've found it helps to have a better grasp on what's really out there. One of my favorite writers was the late John Gardner, author of *Grendel*, *October Light*, *Mickelsson's Ghosts*, and others. His books, *The Art of Fiction*, *On Becoming a Novelist*, and *On Moral Fiction* are required reading for serious writers. In his book *The Art of Fiction*, he gave some advice that, although primarily for writers, it's just as true for other creative endeavors. In a world of puffy, cheesy creative quotes, this is some of the best, most realistic, and encouraging advice I've ever heard:

> *Though learning to write takes time and a great deal of practice, writing up to the world's ordinary standards is fairly easy. As a matter of fact, most of the books one finds in drugstores, supermarkets, and even small-town public libraries are not well written at all; a smart chimp with a good creative writing teacher and a real love of sitting around banging a typewriter could have written books vastly more interesting and elegant. Most grown-ups' behavior, when you come right down to it, is decidedly second-class. People don't drive their cars as well, or wash their ears as well, or eat as well, or even play the harmonica as well as they would if they had sense. This is not to say people are terrible and should be replaced by machines; people are excellent and admirable creatures; efficiency isn't everything.*

> *But for the serious young writer who wants to get published,*
> *it is encouraging to know that most of the writers out there*
> *are pushovers.*[7]

That quote always gives me a shot in the arm, and I'd bet it's true
across all creative endeavors.

DON'T BE AFRAID TO SAY, "I DON'T KNOW."

Before we leave this section, it's important to overcome the fear of
saying, "I don't know." I've been in countless creative meetings where
someone was asked about an issue, and although they had no clue,
they were too embarrassed to admit it. In most cases, they responded
with something everyone in the room knew was wrong or made up
something so crazy they looked like an idiot.

Way too often in modern business, competition makes us feel that
we can't ask for help. We think it will show weakness, and as a result,
we lie. We try to make everyone think we can handle everything when
the truth is, we have lots of questions. And when it comes to generating
ideas on a deadline, we simply don't have the time to wander around in
the dark to cover up the fact that we don't know something.

**Insecure people are terrified that people around
them will think they don't know what they're doing.
But people who are secure in their abilities or career
have the confidence to ask for help. As a result, they
find answers and move ahead of everyone else.**

---

7   John Champlin Gardner, *The Art of Fiction: Notes on Craft for Young Writers* (New York:
Vintage, 1991).

If you struggle with insecurity or with asking for help, this week make a concerted effort to admit that you don't know. Ask for help. For some of you, it will be tough—maybe horrifying. But the truth is, the people around you aren't out to destroy you (well, maybe a few). Once the good ones realize you're honest and vulnerable, they'll be more than willing to help you find the answers.

Don't cut yourself off from the help of the people around you. Start admitting that you don't know all the answers, and see what happens.

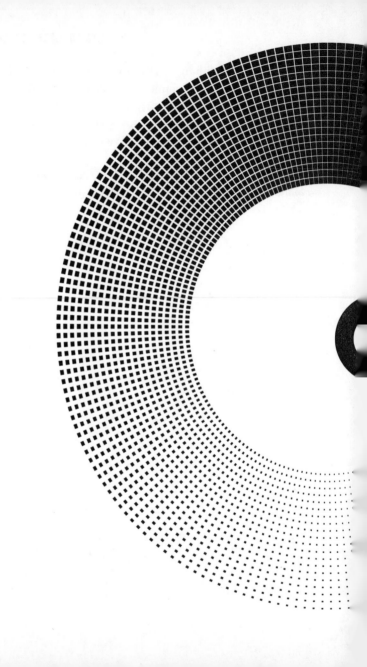

CHAPTER 9

DO WE BECOME LESS CREATIVE AS WE GET OLDER?

How old would you be if you didn't know how old you was?

—Satchel Paige, baseball legend

Before we begin the *method* of creating ideas on a deadline, it's important to put an end to the myth that age diminishes creativity. There's a frustrating and incorrect idea out there that to be creative means to be young. Hollywood and the celebrity machine are big culprits because of their obsessive desire to reach youthful audiences. And even in advertising, business, social, and nonprofit spaces, there's also a strong bias in favor of young people when it comes to creativity.

If you're an older creative professional, you know what I mean.

The problem is, there's no science to support that idea. A *Psychology Today* study reported in 2009 that creativity doesn't diminish with age. Shelley H. Carson, PhD, in her article "Creativity and the Aging Brain," concluded, "I suggest that we change our expectations of the elderly. Instead of referring to 'the aging problem,' we should expect our seniors to be productive throughout the lifespan."

Economist David Galenson, author of *Old Masters and Young Geniuses: The Two Life Cycles of Artistic Creativity,* views the issue not as "creative versus not creative," but through the lens of different approaches to creativity at different times of life.[8]

Tom Jacobs wrote about 221 famous painters of the 19th and 20th centuries and compared their total lifespans with the year they created their most highly valued work. On average, the painters produced those pieces when they were 41.92 years old; they had lived just under 62 percent of their total lives.

Drake Baer reported in *Fast Company* that 42 percent of Robert Frost's poems were written after the age of fifty. For Wallace Stevens, it was 49 percent. For William Carlos Williams, it was 44 percent. This extends into other fields: Oliver Sacks, the beloved psychologist, was super creative into his 80s. The sculptor Louis Bourgeois said, "I am a long-distance runner. It takes me years and years and years to produce what I do"—and she did her best work in her 80s.

Emine Saner reported in *The Guardian* on acclaimed artist Paula Rego:
Working in her studio for up to twelve hours a day, six days a week, Paula Rego's creative drive is as intense as ever. "Even if I'm tired when I start working, by the end I have a lot of energy,"

---

8   David W. Galenson, *Old Masters and Young Geniuses: The Two Life Cycles of Artistic Creativity* (Princeton: Princeton University Press, 2006).

*she says. "It's very important for women to keep working." At the
age of seventy-three, she has never considered retiring.*

In advertising, older creative professionals are everywhere. One of
my favorites is Lee Clow, longtime creative director, and more recently
chairman emeritus, TBWA\Media Arts Lab, who recently retired
(theoretically). Lee created the legendary 1984 Apple commercial
and worked closely with Steve Jobs for thirty years. He's done breakthrough advertising for brands like Nike, Nissan, Olympia Beer, Pacific
Northwest Bell, Pioneer Electronics, Pizza Hut, Porsche, and Yamaha.
He's considered a creative guru, and even after officially "retiring" at
seventy-eight, he'll be surfing more, but I have a feeling he's not completely walking away from advertising.

The bottom line is that creativity isn't related to age as much as it is hunger—the never-ending desire to observe, learn, and grow.

As long as you're exploring, trying new things, reflecting about what
could be, and not afraid to fail, you'll stay creative as long as you desire.
As Carolyn Gregoire has written:

*Creative people are insatiably curious—they generally opt to live
the examined life, and even as they get older, maintain a sense
of curiosity about life. Whether through intense conversation
or solitary mind-wandering, creatives look at the world around
them and want to know why, and how, it is the way it is.
That's not an age decision; that's a mindset decision.*

81

PART 3

THE METHOD
THE ART OF CREATIVE EXTENSIONS

After all, most writing is done away from the typewriter, away from the desk. I'd say it occurs in the quiet silent moments, while you're walking or shaving or playing a game, or whatever, or even talking to someone you're not vitally interested in. You're working, your mind is working, on this problem in the back of your head.

—**Henry Miller, novelist**

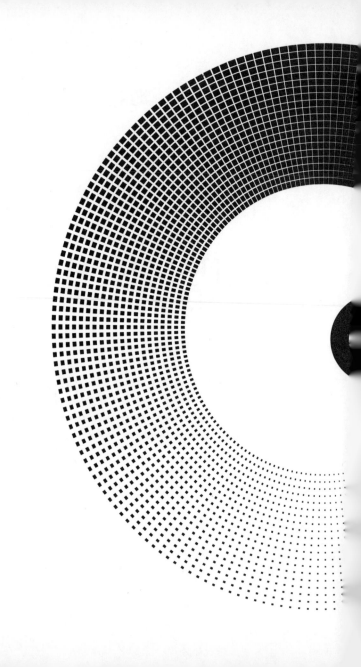

83

CHAPTER 10

START WITH CLARITY

Oftentimes pressure comes because there's not enough time. But that can also be a blessing in disguise. When there's no time, you can't overthink it, and there's no time for others to meddle and water it down. It allows for clarity of vision.

—Marc Levy, SVP, Insights and
Creative Catalyst, Ketchum

In my experience, poor communication may be the single greatest reason creative people fail. In advertising, perhaps the creative brief isn't clear. In a meeting, we don't ask enough questions. With an assignment, we don't drill down to what really matters. Early in my creative career, I was stung a few times because I delivered brilliant creative solutions for the wrong problems. In my excitement to win the project, I simply failed to clarify what the client really needed. One of my great weaknesses is that I care more about how much gas is in the car than what's actually under the hood.

Let's get moving! We can worry about the details later.

But that usually ends in disaster.

You know the reasons. We're enthusiastic and want to get to work. We assume too much. We don't want to look inexperienced or stupid. We need to convey confidence. We have our own ideas of what the client needs.

In other words, we're thinking about holding up the trophy before actually being declared the winner.

> ### *There are few things more powerful than a life lived with passionate clarity.*
> —ERWIN MCMANUS, DESIGNER, FILMMAKER,
> ENTREPRENEUR, AND PASTOR

The question is, at the beginning of a great challenge, how can we achieve clarity on the project? How can we be sure we're heading in the right direction with all the information we need to hit the target?

1) **When it comes to clarity, take the responsibility yourself.** In the end, you can't blame the client, your boss, or anyone else if you didn't get the information you need. Even when they aren't good communicators, you need to step up. Stop blaming, and start taking responsibility.

   Achieving clarity isn't about luck, being in the right place, or having a smart client or boss. Clarity is a decision. You have to decide that it's important enough to ask more questions, do more research, question assumptions, and have the confidence to move forward.

   Clarity is up to you.

2) **Learn people skills.** Some creatives, in an awkward effort to achieve clarity, become jerks. They question the boss or client in

demeaning ways or come off as superior to everyone else in the room. Asking the right questions in the right way is a skill that should be taken very seriously.

I had a high school football coach who said, "Tact is the ability to tell a man to go to hell and make him happy he's on his way." The same is true about clarity. Sometimes achieving it requires tough questions, but they should always be asked in a gracious and nonthreatening way.

Being a jerk will always come back to haunt you.

3) **Simplicity always wins.** Nobody cares how smart you are or how complex you can make a project sound. The key to clarity is making it simple to understand. Even the ancient world understood this. The Old Testament book of Psalms says, "The law of the LORD is perfect, reviving the soul; the testimony of the LORD is sure, making wise the simple" (Psalms 19:7 ESV).

Andrew Edmiston is the managing director of IM Group Limited, an automobile, property, and finance group based in the United Kingdom. It's a highly respected, family-owned company, founded by Lord Robert Edmiston in 1976. Some years ago, Andrew's team purchased a Japanese vehicle franchise in the UK from an importer that had been struggling. Although the model was very popular with older customers, they decided to go after a younger market. So they invested an enormous amount of time, money, and creative work into youthful marketing and advertising in an effort to make the car more attractive to younger people.

Needless to say, it didn't get the results they expected.

Looking closer, they quickly discovered the reasons the car was so popular with older customers revolved around *simple* things, like an uncomplicated door hinge design that allowed the door to open ninety degrees, making it easier for older customers to get in and out. And it didn't take long to see that there were many similar details on the car.

And the truth is, as older customers eventually stop buying cars, younger customers age and start looking for the same features. Andrew recalls the revelation this way: "The lesson I learned is that what seems obvious is often difficult (trying to pioneer a new market for a product that's really not relevant to that market) but when you notice the details, the right answer is often very simple, and completely obvious when you really understand what's important."

Andrew Edmiston learned the power of simplicity and clarity.

> *Making the simple complicated is commonplace; making the complicated simple, awesomely simple, that's creativity.*
> —CHARLES MINGUS, JAZZ MUSICIAN AND COMPOSER

Before John F. Kennedy became president, he was a captain of PT-109—a patrol torpedo boat fighting the Japanese navy during World War II. During one run, PT-109 was cut in half by a Japanese destroyer, and after a difficult swim for survival, Kennedy and his sailors eventually were rescued. Later, when reporters asked him about how he became a hero, his reply was simple: "It was involuntary. They sank my boat."

Walt Whitman was right when he wrote, "Simplicity is the glory of expression."

No matter how complex the project, the skill that brings the most clarity is the ability to reduce the problem, challenge, or task to its simplest terms.

That's the place to start.

CHAPTER 11

GET YOUR LIFE IN ORDER

Your mind is for having ideas, not holding them.

—David Allen, *Getting Things Done*

Now that you have clarity on the project or challenge you're facing, let's talk about the method—ideas and techniques that have worked for me, and I believe will work for you as well. However, you don't have to apply every technique to every challenge. One or two is often all it takes to unlock a brilliant idea. So feel free to adapt and experiment to find the right priorities for the creative challenges you face.

I mentioned earlier that in the twenty-first century, we've almost become slaves to *the cult of productivity*. What began in the Industrial Age to help a large workforce become more efficient has today shifted to our *personal* space where productivity apps, team software, and tracking programs have exploded. As a result, *productivity* has become an obsession.

And in some cultures, it's deadly. I directed a TV commercial for a large Asian advertising agency, and while talking to the creative director on the set, he shared that the pressure at the agency was enormous. After a full workday, employees were typically expected to work extensive overtime and then take clients out for dinner and drinks, often until after midnight. That level of productivity took a toll. Workers committing suicide because of those outrageous demands were not unusual, and he admitted they had hired seven full-time psychiatrists on staff just to deal with the mental and emotional problems.

While you may not be under that kind of pressure, you probably do own at least one task manager or to-do app, print notebook, or use another method in an often-failed attempt just to keep track of everything you have to accomplish.

Speaking to the World Creativity Forum, John Cleese of *Monty Python* fame described it this way:

> *If you're racing around all day, ticking things off a list, looking at your watch, making phone calls, and generally just keeping all the balls in the air, you are not going to have any creative ideas.*

That's why more and more research indicates that a productivity mindset isn't the mindset for great creative work. Under pressure to be more productive, our mind focuses on details (the checklist) and not on the big picture issues that fuel creativity.

And daydream? Forget it. My entire life has been a relentless march of parents, teachers, and bosses trying to stop me from daydreaming. All my years in school, growing up in church, sitting at home, and later at the office, I was taught that daydreaming accomplishes nothing and is a one-way ticket to Loserville. But now, more and more studies indicate that without times of personal reflection, deep thinking, and daydreaming, we'll never open up the deep wells of creativity.

Rahaf Harfoush, author of *Hustle & Float: Reclaim your Creativity* and *Thrive in a World Obsessed with Work,* puts it this way:

> *According to a team of researchers from the University of Southern California, those episodes when our minds wander are essential mental states that help us develop our identity, process social interactions, and even influence our internal moral compass. When we daydream, our brains shift their focus from the outside world to a rich inner landscape where we can explore our desires, dreams, and hopes while working out our tensions and conflicts. We need the time to reflect and think and to try to make sense of the world and our place in it.*

It took me years to overcome the *productivity mindset* and even longer to create space for serious, focused creative time. However, that's not to say some productivity techniques are necessarily a problem. In fact, they are the tools that can open up those creative blocks of time. *How* we use those tools can actually help us build walls that protect our scheduled times of deeper focus.

To accomplish that, the first thing I recommend is to clear the deck of as many distractions as possible. Writer and business consultant Stephen Covey says, "The key is not to prioritize what's on your schedule, but to schedule your priorities." In other words, decide what's important to you, and *get organized*. Today, there's a wide range of options to help, from productivity apps for your computer and mobile device, to print notebooks, or even a simple notepad. There is no perfect method, so whatever works best is whatever works best for you.

> ***Deadlines and the lack of deadlines—there are times when I need not worry about when something needs to be done, there are other times I have to have a deadline. I need to relax, I need to work like crazy, I need to be organized, I need to be disorganized. Sometimes I have a gut feel, I'm a bit uncomfortable because things are a little too***

> *organized. Sometimes you need some disorganization to*
> *force you to take a wrong turn and see where it leads.*
> —CHRIS RUNCO, WALT DISNEY IMAGINEER

Perhaps you like giant random piles of papers on your desk, but I can't work that way. I need a bit more organization to help me set up my creative time. Personally, I admit that I have a thing for to-do lists. Not that I'm even remotely detail-oriented, but I love working with apps that help me sort and organize my projects and ideas. I've always been a follower of David Allen's "Getting Things Done" concept, but I have one significant problem: I'm a big idea person, so I'm always coming up with things I should do: films I should make, ideas for books, client tasks, and more. I looked at my to-do list once, and it had 783 items on it.

When I looked at that crushing list, I just shut down. It was overwhelming and depressing. I was paralyzed and getting nothing done. That's when a revelation hit. When I looked at the 783 items on my task list, I realized that the vast majority weren't actual *things to do*; they were *ideas*—mostly ideas for future projects. They weren't actual tasks I needed to accomplish anytime soon, and very few were urgent.

So I edited my to-do list into *actionable steps* versus *creative ideas*. When I did that, my to-do list became much more manageable and realistic.

We all have "ideas," but don't confuse that with actionable steps we need to take today or tomorrow. Big difference. A 783-item task list will only make you curl up into a fetal position. But if you understand the difference between a *to-do* list and an *idea* list, then your future looks brighter.

THE NOT TO-DO LIST

This is also a good time to mention that when it comes to carving out creative time, "not-to-do" lists are often as effective as to-do lists. The reason is simple: what you *don't* do determines what you *can* do. A simple list of things on my not-to-do list would include:

- **I don't answer the phone if I don't know the person or recognize the number.** I have friends who feel absolutely compelled to answer the phone every time it rings. That may be the single greatest way to interrupt your creativity, waste time, and distract your focus. Be more intentional about letting calls go to voicemail and deal with them later when you're not in creative mode.
- **Avoid meetings with no agenda or end time.** I've had numerous clients over the years who regularly scheduled meetings lasting six or more hours. Usually held with the senior leadership team, they go on and on—often wasting an entire day and exhausting the participants. One notorious nonprofit's monthly leadership and marketing meetings extend literally for two solid days at a time.

I'd rather visit the dentist.

When it comes to meetings, human beings simply can't focus their attention for so long. After about forty minutes at a stretch, even the best people start mentally wandering, opening email, staring out the window, playing with their phone, and checking out. Just notice the faces around the table as you near the first-hour mark, and watch how they start disengaging. From that point on, anything you attempt at the meeting will only have limited results, and effectiveness starts to quickly erode.

Meetings aren't for processing—they're for decisions.

All-day meetings happen because people don't come prepared and expect to do their processing (or thinking) at the meeting itself. All that does is waste everyone's time. The reason you gather all these leaders together isn't to watch everyone think—it's to arrive at a decision.

So when your time comes to speak, give your recommendation for the subject at hand, provide no more than a one-minute explanation, and then hand everyone a "fact sheet" with the details. The fact sheet is the process. It's how you came to your conclusion. You did your homework, so you don't have to bore everyone to death with the details. For those in the room that need more detail, they're welcome to read it at their leisure. For the rest, let's agree or disagree with your recommendation and move on.

Start every meeting with an agenda, and do your best to avoid meetings without one.

An agenda gets everyone on the same page, shows them what to prepare for, and indicates when the meeting will end. This is important even for one-on-one personal meetings. At the very least, drop an email or text message to the person you're meeting with ahead of time just to let him or her know what you want to accomplish when you're together.

I took a meeting one time with a designer who'd waited weeks to see me. Nice guy who wanted to talk about a particular project—at least that's what I thought. But once he came into my office, he had nothing to say. He hadn't done his homework, didn't have questions prepared, and didn't know how I could help. We just sat there doing small talk, and I finally had to ask, "How can I help you? Why are we having this meeting?"

He didn't have an answer.

If you schedule a meeting with another professional to pitch a project, ask for advice, or network—come prepared. Write up some questions, have an agenda, and know what you want the meeting to accomplish. Better yet—email them ahead of time, so the other person can prepare for the meeting. It will be far more productive than just sitting around looking clueless.

Stop checking your email constantly during the day. Experienced professionals know that when you're focusing on creative work, having your email, text messages, or notifications running in the background will kill your productivity. You can't focus when you're constantly being interrupted by messages. Use time outside your creative block to check on your messages and update other responsibilities. Please take this seriously. Best-selling author Tim Ferris says responding constantly to emails and other messages is like being hooked up to a *cocaine pellet dispenser,* and he's exactly right. Few things will destroy your creativity more than allowing yourself to be available for a constant barrage of notifications, texts, and emails.

Ron Friedman, writing in the *Harvard Business Review,* wrote that "Shifting our attention from one task to another, as we do when we're monitoring email while trying to read a report or craft a presentation, disrupts our concentration and saps our focus." And all these distractions take their toll on our productivity. He cites a University of California-Irvine study that indicates trying to get back to your original momentum after these interruptions can take more than twenty minutes. So how many of these interruptions does it take to completely ruin your day?

Plus, other studies show that multitasking is a total myth. As Friedman says:

A more accurate account of what happens when we tell ourselves we're multitasking is that we're rapidly switching between activities, degrading our clarity, and depleting our mental energy. And the consequences can be surprisingly serious. An experiment conducted at the University of London found that we lose as many as ten IQ points when we allow our work to be interrupted by seemingly benign distractions like emails and text messages.

IDEAS ON A DEADLINE

When you're up against a deadline, brilliant ideas don't happen when you've lost ten IQ points because you refuse to turn off the distractions.

Multitasking—as in checking email, listening to music, watching TV, or talking to a friend when you're doing creative work is a disaster. People still confidently tell me they can handle it, and some try to convince me that it actually makes them more creative. But I haven't found a single study that indicates multitasking helps you do anything positive.

It only helps you do many things badly.

Much of a typical week for creative professionals consists of returning calls, responding to email, meetings, and more. But if you're spending most of your day working from your task list, your creative time will suffer.

Productivity techniques can be helpful as long as they don't become an end in themselves. If your task list, calendar, project management system, or whatever else you use is able to help schedule and protect your creative time, then go for it. But constantly check to see that productivity techniques haven't highjacked your creative time.

For me, that's a never-ending battle.

As creative professionals, we need sustained, focused creative time that's free from distractions and interruptions. In the distracted world we live in, this is more difficult than ever to accomplish, but without it, the breakthrough ideas will rarely happen.

CHAPTER 12

THE BENEFIT OF CREATIVE EXTENSIONS

POURING GASOLINE ON A FLAME . . .

*Experts are those who have learned how best to marshal
and apply extra-neural resources to the task before them.*

— **Annie Murphy Paul,** *The Extended Mind*

n her excellent book, *The Extended Mind: The Power of Thinking
Outside the Brain*, Annie Murphy Paul makes the case that for too
long, scientists have treated the brain as a disembodied, solitary

organ. She calls it a "brain in a vat."[9] For much of history, they've assumed that our thinking, learning, and ideas all come from the brain and have rarely considered the role the rest of the body plays in how we process ideas.

In this section of the book, we'll talk about how leaving the office, walking, rest, to-do lists, an exterior crisis, the atmosphere of a room, and much more can impact how we learn, how we process, and how we generate ideas—especially when we're facing a deadline.

But those myths about the brain being the solitary source of our ideas persist.

That's why creative writers, designers, and other thinkers sit for hours at their desks and come up with nothing when a brisk walk, a short nap, a hot bath, or a conversation with a colleague might trigger something extraordinary.

The truth is, our brains are limited, and in today's digital age there's growing evidence we're pushing the limits of what our brains can process.

No matter how high your IQ, the way you were raised, your genetics, years of experience, or the number of graduate degrees after your name, your brain is a finite organ, and especially in today's cluttered, distracted, digital culture, it can only handle so much information. Our brains are limited, and in today's digital age there's growing evidence we're pushing the limits of what our brains can process.

You're probably familiar with the famous Microsoft study that indicated our attention span is about eight seconds (or the same length

---

9 Annie Murphy Paul, *The Extended Mind: The Power of Thinking Outside the Brain* (Boston: Houghton Mifflin Harcourt, 2021).

as that of a goldfish.) To a great degree, that's because we're simply being overwhelmed with information. Some researchers report the typical person sees about ten thousand media messages per day, and the amount of time we spend on social media is staggering.

At the same time, it's sobering to realize how quickly this has happened. It's been said that when we read just seven days of a daily newspaper (if anyone reads newspapers anymore) we've read more information than a typical person just one hundred years ago read during their *entire lifetime*. Add on the fact that a century ago, reading wasn't forced to compete with TV, movies, the internet, social media, podcasting, and a host of other media options.

So to think that in about one hundred years the average person went from reading the equivalent of seven editions of a newspaper over their entire lives to being bombarded with ten thousand messages a day is a massive shift. Some researchers report that 90 percent of all the information created in the history of the world has been generated in the last two years!

The onslaught is largely due to the growth of the internet—and the growing impact of video. As far back as 2012, ComScore reported the average viewer watched nearly twenty-two hours of video in a single month, and that percentage has been climbing with no sign of letting up. By 2020, that had grown to an average of six hours and fifty-nine minutes *per day* consuming content, which includes phone, TV, and other forms of digital media. For those who may be skeptics, on your next airline flight, count how many passengers are watching movies or videos on their devices versus reading a book.

With video, those viewing hours were usually broken into many short videos, with each being viewed for just a few minutes at a time—which continues to shorten our attention span. The bottom line is that we've reached a level of media consumption where the human brain can only understand and process so much.

IDEAS ON A DEADLINE

Dickens didn't have Google, Mozart didn't have GarageBand, Charlie Chaplin didn't have YouTube, Walt Disney had no cell phone, and the Roman army didn't have GPS. We have incredible technology.
—DON HAHN, PRODUCER OF *THE LION KING* AND *BEAUTY AND THE BEAST*

In today's world, where our brains are overtaxed, we're also surrounded by "thinking tools," and yet creative professionals rarely take full advantage of those resources. Our physical bodies, the technology at our fingertips, our surroundings, the people around us—all can contribute to the process of creativity and expand what our normal mind is capable of accomplishing.

Think of how scents can trigger powerful memories and emotions, and yet how often do we consider enhancing the odors and scents at our office or workplace?

A personally designed workspace makes us more relaxed and comfortable, yet how often do we sit in cubicles or offices that someone else designed—or with no design at all?

Recall how much your thinking changes when you're in certain locations. There is evidence that views of nature can significantly improve academic performance with students. Australian researchers discovered that even a small "micro-break" looking out across a meadow enhanced the results of cognitive tests over other participants that looked out at a concrete wall.

The quality and creativity associated with children's play is better when it's done outside rather than indoors. Even a short stroll through a park can reset our thinking and spark new ideas.

What about people? Have you noticed that you're generally more creative when you're around certain people than when you spend time with others? Some friends inspire and motivate you while others seem to suck the very life out of you.

Maybe we should be spending time with more inspiring people.

It's time we became serious about using the world outside our brain to enhance our creative thinking.

I learned long ago that I'm easily distracted, so to maximize my creative time, I installed translucent windows in my office that let the light in but hide the outside world. I can't have music playing or a TV turned on—it's just too distracting. My assistant made a sign with a quote from the movie *The Wizard of Oz* that hangs on my door: "Nobody gets in to see the wizard. Not nobody. Not nohow."

I always felt a little guilty until I recently discovered that best-selling novelist Judith Krantz revealed:

> *I have a sign on the door that says: DO NOT COME IN. DO NOT KNOCK. DO NOT SAY HELLO. DO NOT SAY "I'M LEAVING." DO NOT SAY ANYTHING UNLESS THE HOUSE IS ON FIRE. . . . Also, telephone's off.*

You get my drift. When faced with a great creative challenge, we often depend too much on our overtaxed brain and fail to consider what these and other extensions can help us accomplish. This section is a look at those extensions—some of which you may have considered and others probably not. This isn't a *medical prescription*; it's a *menu*, so feel free to experiment and explore what works for you.

CHAPTER 13

START WITH A BLANK PAGE

My perfect day is sitting in a room with some blank paper. That's heaven. That's gold, and anything else is just a waste of time.

—Cormac McCarthy, novelist

James Webb Young's career was part of the foundation that built the legendary *Mad Men* era of advertising. He was a vice president of J. Walter Thompson Advertising Agency and became the first chairman of The Advertising Council. During his career as a copywriter, he developed a five-step model of the creative process which eventually became a short book called *A Technique for Producing Ideas*. Even after all these years, Young's five steps are still considered the standard process for developing innovative thinking:

1) **Gather raw material.** Ask questions, read, do research, interview the right people, visit the factory—literally anything that will give you all the background information you need to jumpstart your thinking.

2) **Work over that material.** Young calls it "The process of masticating these materials, as you would food that you are preparing for digestion." For most people, this is the hard work of creativity. Play around with your information, try alternative ideas, start writing, make false starts, agonize, sweat it.

3) **Walk away.** This is the "incubation" stage of the process. Do something completely different, so your subconscious mind can work on the challenge. Detective Sherlock Holmes would play the violin or smoke his pipe. (He also had a little problem with opium.) As you'll see a bit later in the book, many creative thinkers take walks.

   Pick up a hobby. Take a shower. Let your mind wander.

4) **Aha! The eureka moment happens.** As Young said, "Out of nowhere, the idea will appear."

5) **Shape the idea into what will actually work.** Oddly enough, this is where many creative people fail because they don't have the patience or the discipline to tweak, sand down the edges, and make the idea fit into what's needed. Whether it's an advertising billboard, a real estate presentation, a speech, or the offensive strategy for a football team, it has to be molded into a final product that works.[10]

One of my favorite periods in the creative process is gathering the raw material. I absolutely love reading up on the history of the project, exploring what's worked (or not worked) in the past, interviewing people involved, visiting the location, and reading books that will help me set the stage. Honestly, that's the easy part because I'm exploring, the information is fascinating, and there is very little pressure at this stage.

---

10 James Webb Young, *A Technique for Producing Ideas* (New York: McGraw-Hill, 2007).

*As chefs, especially pastry chefs, your creativity plays such
an important part in your daily work. We truly do have a
blank canvas to work with every time we create a new dish.*
—JOHNNY IUZZINI, AUTHOR AND PASTRY CHEF

However, the first big challenge is the blank page. How and where do you start—particularly when the deadline is standing there in the distance laughing at you? Here are a few key things that help me when I'm staring at a blank page:

1) **Ask what's true about this project.** Particularly in the advertising and marketing world, there's a lot of hype, exaggeration, and fluff around products and ideas, so it's helpful to drill down to what's really true. Winston Churchill said, "The truth is incontrovertible. Malice may attack it, ignorance may deride it, but in the end, there it is." Regardless of what people may think of the project or product, they can't argue with the truth. Figure that out, and you have a place to start.

2) **Write down everything.** One of my favorite quotes is from Linus Pauling: "The best way to get a good idea is to get a lot of ideas." Working in Hollywood, I've met two kinds of people. One group has spent their entire career pitching one big idea. It may be a movie, TV series, or other dream project that they've wrapped their entire professional career around. They've put all their eggs in that one basket.

   The second group is constantly generating ideas. They have multiple presentations, scripts, and pitches standing by. They're always in creative mode and can adapt on a moment's notice.

   In my experience, the second group is the one that works the most.

   Culture, trends, styles, and people change, so your goal is to always be in idea mode, and keep that flow working.

3) **Embrace the suck.** That's what Luke Sullivan and Edward Boches recommend in their excellent book *Hey Whipple, Squeeze This: The Classic Guide to Creating Great Ads*. They describe it like this: "If your brand has some sort of obvious shortcoming (it's ugly or tastes bad), try seeing what'll happen if you address that directly and really own it. Denying it is inauthentic, and as long as the benefits outweigh the negatives, it's all good. Plus, customers will love you for your candor and transparency."[11]

The greatest embrace the suck example of all time may be the classic rental car campaign: *We're Avis. We're only number two. So we try harder.*

4) **Don't be afraid of conflict.** Where would Luke Skywalker be without Darth Vader? Where would Batman be without The Joker? Where would Harry Potter be without Lord Voldemort? Without conflict, there is no struggle, no growth, and no victory. Maybe your villain is your competition, something you discover in a focus group, or an earlier version of your own idea.

As I write this, legendary TV pitchman Ron Popeil just passed away. Ron put direct-response infomercials on the map, and I saw his mind-bending influence up close and personal because my father-in-law had a garage full of stuff he'd purchased from Popeil's television infomercials. Products like The Pocket Fisherman, Veg-O-Matic, Showtime Rotisserie, Ronco Knives, Mr. Microphone, and much more. I even directed a series of TV commercials with a famous actor who used Popeil's spray-on Hair in a Can on his bald spot.

A really big part of Ron's pitch was comparing his own products to "inferior" competitors. He always had a villain, and that's what made him so magnetic.

---

11 Luke Sullivan and Edward Boches, *Hey Whipple, Squeeze This: The Classic Guide to Creating GREAT ADS: Includes Digital, Social, and Emerging Media* (Hoboken: Wiley, 2016).

5) **Ask a better question.** When facing a creative challenge, the simple question "Why?" can completely change the direction of your thinking. Educational consultant Peter Block says, "Getting the question right may be the most important thing we can do."

The problem is that throughout most of our lives we're discouraged from asking questions. I remember how often our young daughters were asking questions about everything, and although it drove me crazy, I realized their need to understand the world. In school, most teachers get frustrated with students who are constantly asking questions. And certainly in business, those who routinely question the boss tend to not get promoted.

We need to overcome that lifetime of imprinting and get back to the joy of asking better questions. The best questioners aren't satisfied with existing reality, and as a result, are often the most creative.

Whether you're pondering a creative challenge, your career, or your personal life, we can never ask too many questions, and the best place to start is with "Why?" Approach every new challenge like a beginner, and never be afraid to start asking questions to discover the best answers.

The right questions can reframe the challenge and open doors we never noticed before. The greatest teachers and philosophers rarely lecture; they ask questions—the kind of questions that make people rethink their presuppositions.

Better questions can completely transform your creative results.

6) **The most important thing is to start.** Write a word or phrase, draw a line, just do something. Artist Nathan Oliveira said, "All art is a series of recoveries from the first line." In other words, you can change it as much as you like, but you can't change what's not there. Even if it's nonsense, jot it down.

The start of a new creative challenge isn't the time to make history, be amazing, or change the world. The point of this stage is to get the raw material in words, sketches, ideas, or random thoughts that you can build from.

Particularly when the deadline is looming, the best thing you can possibly do is to get it down. Start. Sketch. Whatever. You'll be amazed at how much that opens a creative door.

Artist Vincent van Gogh said,

Just slap something on it when you see a blank canvas staring at you with a sort of imbecility. You don't know how paralyzing it is, that stare from a blank canvas that says to the painter, "You can't do anything. . . ." Many painters are afraid of the blank canvas, but the blank canvas is afraid of the truly passionate painter who dares—and who has once broken the spell of "you can't."

CHAPTER 14

WRITE IT DOWN!

Sometimes I have a good idea, something I wish I could remember, and instead of writing it down, commit it to my memory only to disappear when I needed it. Write your ideas as they come, if you wait it will be too long and you may not recover it. It may get destroyed as it is to seed to and fro in the ever-rushing river of our thoughts.

—**Bangambiki Habyarimana**, *Pearls Of Eternity*

Novelist E. M. Forster said, "How do I know what I think until I see what I say?" I never understood the brilliance of that statement until I was at a Christmas party, and I encountered an idea that changed my life. I was talking to a man I'd never met before who I soon discovered was a successful entrepreneur from South Africa. After some initial chitchat, I asked him how he started in business. His face brightened up, and he told me this story:

Years ago, I was a regular guy at a normal job just making ends meet. One night, my wife asked me to go shopping with her, and although I hate shopping, I love my wife more, so I joined her. After an hour or so at the mall, I was tired, so decided to sit on a bench while she went into another store to look at dresses.

While I was sitting on the bench, I started noticing young people using their cell phones. It was back in the early days of mobile, and most of them were using a radical new invention called a "flip phone." As I watched, out of the blue, the thought occurred to me how fun it would be if they could use their favorite songs as ringtones on their phones. I had never even considered that before, and at the time, people only had a handful of different ring choices—most of them pretty terrible.

So I hastily pulled a pen out of my pocket, found a discarded brochure on the bench, and wrote the idea down on the back. About that same moment, my wife called for me to come into the store and look at a dress. I stuffed the note into my jacket pocket, walked into the store, and promptly forgot all about it.

About six months later, I went to the closet, put on that same jacket, and found that crumpled note in the pocket. I immediately remembered that night at the shopping mall and realized that using popular songs as ringtones still made a lot of sense. I started small—I bought the rights to five songs, built a computer server, and made a deal with a local cell phone company. A year or so later, I sold that company for $70 million.

That's when he looked into my eyes and said: "And here's the thing; if I hadn't written that idea down, I would have completely forgotten about it."

That was a $70 million idea that he jotted down on a discarded brochure, but unless he had written it, its value was zero. Think of that for a minute, and think of all the ideas that pop into your head that you never take the time to write down.

I later discovered that he wasn't the first to invent using songs as ringtones, but he was the first in his part of the world to implement the technology and was bought out by one of the large mobile phone companies at the time.

Most importantly, I've never forgotten that story and have never been without a pen and paper since.

Ideas are the most fragile things in the world. If you don't write them down, they'll completely disappear.

Composer Ludwig van Beethoven was famous for always carrying a pencil and a few sheets of paper in case a musical idea suddenly came to mind. Computer graphics pioneer Ivan Sutherland went so far as to say, "It's not an idea until you write it down." How often have you awakened in the middle of the night with a brilliant idea, but instead of writing it down, you left it to memory, only to find you'd forgotten about it the next morning? We get ideas in the strangest places—driving, in the shower, in our sleep, during church, on the golf course, in meetings—and one thing is always true: if we don't write them down, they're gone.

I actually believe that most people don't struggle coming up with great ideas under pressure. The problem is they're not writing them down when they happen.

Before you do anything further, commit to never being without a tool for recording your ideas. You may prefer old fashioned pen and paper, or recording on a phone, or something else. Whatever it is, stick to it.

Because I've learned from bitter experience that memory can't be trusted, there's a framework I've developed for dealing with ideas, whether or not I'm under a deadline. In my case, I use a few different methods because of the nature of my work and my travel schedule. They may work for you, or perhaps you'll come up with a better plan, but here's how I break them down.

CAPTURING IDEAS

I start with two simple things: notecards and an app. I carry notecards and a small pen everywhere I go for jotting things down. They also make great bookmarks, so I can capture ideas when I'm reading. It's the most simple and effective way for me—particularly if I need to sketch a concept. Notecards are inexpensive and can be easily purchased at an office supply store or online. My cards are 3x5, so they easily fit into my pocket, and I have my name, phone, and email address printed at the top which allows me to use them like business cards with space for notes. (Pretty handy, actually).

I also carry a phone app that allows me to enter my email address into the app ahead of time, so I can write or record a note and instantly email it to my account. The recording feature is also good for capturing ideas while driving. Once it's in my email inbox, I can deal with it later. There are other good note-taking apps as well, so experiment, and see what works quickly and efficiently for you.

I can't overemphasize having a dependable method for capturing immediate ideas. With those two methods, I have a solid system for catching the most fleeting thought *whenever* it happens and *wherever* it happens.

PROCESSING IDEAS

The second level is a productivity app and a print notebook. If nothing else, I am an explorer and an experimenter. I fully embrace new techniques, ways of doing things, apps, and more—probably because I get bored easily and love exploring new options (which may explain why I have four different email apps on my computer). When it comes to organized note-taking, I started with a spiral notebook back in college; then, years later gravitated to a computer. I've used various note apps that evolved early, then tried Evernote, but settled on Apple Notes. (It's free, simple, and clean.) To-do apps were the same—I tried Trello, ToDoist, Asana, Microsoft To Do, OmniFocus, and plenty of others before I settled on Things.

But it's not the particular app that matters; it's the idea of writing it down and processing it. Lately, I've decided to migrate much of my work back to my original method—a physical print notebook. Here's why:

1) **My to-do list app (Things) was so easy to use my list grew to be unmanageable.** Yes—a great app allows you to prioritize, but as I mentioned earlier, I have so many ideas, and the to-do list grew so long, I started to ignore it. I'm still going to keep up that long computer list as a dumping ground (I get a lot of ideas), but when it comes to execution, with a print journal, I can more easily focus on what's really important for each day.

2) **More and more research indicates that the act of physical writing engages the brain more deeply and causes us to remember more than simply typing.** In fact, it's been suggested that physically writing things down could improve immune cell activity and reduce antibody counts for people with viruses like Epstein-Barr and AIDS. Some scientists even think physical writing can improve memory and help you sleep.

3) **While there are plenty of sketching apps for my mobile devices, there's nothing like physically sketching ideas out on a piece**

of paper. Some people prefer digital pads, and if that's your preference, then run with it.

4) **I've shifted from taking extensive meeting notes to writing down action steps, so a notebook is perfect for that.** If I have more extensive notes, I'll stick them in Apple Notes.

5) **This may sound old-school, but I'm uncomfortable opening my computer in some client meetings—even if I'm taking notes on it.** Sure, nearly everyone does it these days, but the truth is, at the same time most of those people are also checking email, text messaging, and more. I'm old enough to feel that it's disrespectful to the leader or client, and if you can't go a few hours without checking your email, then you have bigger problems. Just try it—in your next meeting, make notes using a pen and paper, and see if your attention, focus, and creativity don't increase. (After you go through the withdrawal of being unplugged.)

6) **Again—it might be old-school, but reading through my ideas in notebooks is far more inspiring and insightful than scrolling through those same ideas in a computer document.** If the whole point of keeping notes is for later review, then a notebook wins hands down.

SO HOW DO I USE A PRINT NOTEBOOK?

My notebook is a combination of new ideas, project notes, and a to-do list (or action steps). I'm a writer and producer, so I use a combination of writing and sketching in my notebook, although I do far more writing. So here's what I focus on:

1) **An area for the overall project or topic of the day.** It may be a meeting, a video, or writing project, client calls, or a strategy session. I note that at the top with the date and location.

2) **An area for very brief notes or sketches.** As I mentioned, I discovered that after years and years of note-taking, I rarely actually

went back to look at those mountains of notes (sound familiar?), so I switched to action steps.

3) **An area for action steps.** This can also be called a to-do list or task list. This isn't a long list; it has three big things I need to accomplish today, or in other cases, what I'm going to do as a result of this meeting, project, or strategy session.

That's really all I need. So many published notebooks today are filled with "daily affirmations," pre-guided templates for productivity, inspirational quotes, or cute drawings. All that I really need are the three areas above, and over the years, I've tried a wide variety of notebooks. For instance, for ideas and meeting notes I tried the Bullet Journal concept, which is pretty much completely blank. If you have tons of free time to create all your lists and schedules, then great, but most of us have to work for a living.

In the opposite direction, the Passion Planner, and others like the Full Focus Planner, come with predesigned templates and ask me to fill out way too much information—much of which isn't related to my creative work. They're more for organizing your life than organizing your creativity.

I'd encourage you to look at the wide range of print notebooks out there, and find the right one for you.

I've discovered that more and more research backs up my decision to move to a print planner. The Association for Psychological Science reports that taking notes by hand is better than taking notes on a laptop for remembering conceptual information over the long term. Pam Mueller of Princeton University reports that "Our new findings suggest that even when laptops are used as intended—and not for buying things on Amazon during class—they may still be harming academic performance."

Perhaps, most importantly, when it comes to generating ideas on the run, the act of writing goals and tasks down causes me to pause and reflect. My thinking is more clear, and those moments of reflection make a dramatic difference in the quality of my ideas.

I'm not asking you to go cold turkey on your digital life. Continue to work on your laptop or mobile device, check emails on whatever is most convenient, and use a shared online calendar with your team. I still use Things for my personal ideas and to-do list, and our team uses Asana to track our projects as a group. But when it comes to designing your day and accomplishing your goals, from my experience, you can't beat a print planner working in tandem with your apps.

115

CHAPTER 15

FOR THE BEST IDEAS, GO TO THE SOURCE

The patterns are simple, but followed together, they make for a whole that is wiser than the sum of its parts. Go for a walk; cultivate hunches; write everything down, but keep your folders messy; embrace serendipity; make generative mistakes; take on multiple hobbies; frequent coffeehouses and other liquid networks; follow the links; let others build on your ideas; borrow, recycle; reinvent. Build a tangled bank.

—Steven Johnson, *Where Good Ideas Come From: The Natural History of Innovation*

While creative ideas can happen in an office, I like getting out and exploring where the problem lives. Early in my career, a major oil company experienced a horrible explosion at a refinery in south Texas. Multiple people were killed, and it was a public relations nightmare. Their challenge was to win back the public's trust and rebuild, and as that process started, they asked me to write and produce a documentary film telling that story.

I spent a lot of time in my office thinking about what approach I should take but wasn't getting anywhere, so I asked permission to visit the explosion site. Keep in mind that even weeks after the disaster, the authorities had still restricted access to what was left of the refinery, so it took a lot of convincing on my part.

But the minute I walked around the rubble, everything changed. Seeing the curled and melted steel, the little that was left of the refinery, and getting a glimpse of the enormity of rebuilding such a large and complex facility, launched me in a completely different creative direction.

That evening, I went back to my hotel room and started writing.

Since then, I've become an advocate of creative people being on location and visiting where the problem lives. Whenever possible, I even recommend having regular meetings on location. After all, how much does the sterility of a conference room inspire you versus being at the construction site, the hospital, the factory floor, or the historical location?

All the doughnuts in the conference room don't equal seeing the real problem face-to-face.

> *Any time you design a character for a*
> *Disney picture, especially a fairy tale,*
> *it's going to become the definitive design for that*
> *character, so you don't want to hack something out.*
> *You need to put in the kind of care it*
> *warrants if it's going to live in history.*
> —GLEN KEANE, ARTIST AND WALT DISNEY ANIMATOR

The first time I met legendary artist and animator Glen Keane, he had just finished creating Ariel, the mermaid in the Walt Disney Studios movie *The Little Mermaid*. That film had a profound impact on our two daughters, and Glen graciously did an autographed drawing of the character for the girls that we immediately framed (and which may be the most valuable item in our entire house).

Glen was a key element in Disney's transition from the legendary first generation of animators to the next, and he was a driving force at the studio for three decades. Though he's created countless characters over the years, among his best work includes Ratigan in *The Great Mouse Detective*, Ariel in *The Little Mermaid*, Marahute the eagle in *The Rescuers Down Under*, the Beast in *Beauty and the Beast*, Aladdin, and Tarzan, and he supervised the animation in Disney's hit movie *Tangled*. Perhaps more than his amazing accomplishments, Glen has been a respected mentor to a generation of young animators, and his influence in Hollywood and beyond is remarkable.

At our first meeting, I was struck by his passion for traveling and his belief about how important it is for creative people to get out of the office. To prepare for new animation challenges, he spent time in Europe, particularly in Paris, and in preparation for drawing the Beast from Disney's *Beauty and the Beast*, he went to multiple zoos to study how a human prince could potentially look as an animal. He mentioned that Disney animators regularly make field trips and travel extensively for inspiration and insight.

> *Before you open your pad, open five other things.*
> *Your ears, your eyes, and your mind. You'll never be*
> *a good writer of anything if you just sit in your office*
> *and stare at your desk. Your raw material isn't in the*
> *office. It's out in the streets. Look at pictures. Listen to*
> *music. Go to films. See plays. And more importantly,*

look at people. They're those funny things with two
legs we're meant to be writing about, remember.
—JAMES LOWTHER, COPYWRITER AND FOUNDING
PARTNER IN ADVERTISING AGENCY M&C SAATCHI

I was thirty-six years old and had been fired from my job in the Midwest when our family made the decision to move to Los Angeles. We stopped in Las Vegas for a couple of months to live with my in-laws while we scouted LA for the right location and house. During that transition, a longtime family friend, who happened to be a graphic designer, introduced me to the marketing director for the Circus Circus Hotel and Casino. She also led the marketing efforts at other hotels like Excalibur and the Sahara.

She hired me as a freelancer to write advertising copy for the hotels, which included everything from print ads, naming items on the restaurant menus, and even promotional copy for the boat racing team owned by the hotel's CEO.

After a year or two, she presented me with a really interesting challenge.

At that time, Las Vegas was repositioning itself to be "family-friendly," and Circus Circus was opening The Adventure Dome—a giant glass bubble featuring amusement park rides particularly designed for younger kids. It would be one of the world's largest indoor amusement parks, and it was about to be finished, and the hotel desperately needed to name the rides.

I'd never named amusement park rides before, but I gave it a shot. I spent days playing with the possibilities but wasn't really happy with the results—especially since the names needed to excite elementary-school-aged kids.

So I decided to go to the source.

With the permission of our oldest daughter Kelsey's second-grade teacher, I went into her class, described each of the rides, and the kids jumped right in.

"I have a rollercoaster that will take you on a ride through desert mountains."

Some kid in the back shouted out, "Canyon Blaster!"

Check.

"How about another desert ride that spins in circles and goes up and down?"

Another kid blurted out, "Road Runner!"

Check.

"What about a ride that flings you upside down, side to side, and all over the place?"

My daughter Kelsey and a group of her friends screamed, "Chaos!"

Check.

We went down the list until all the rides were named.

I went home, tossed in a few ideas of my own, and the next day I presented the names to the Circus Circus marketing team; they didn't change a single one.

It's been more than twenty-five years since that happened, and recently, Kathleen and I took Kelsey, her husband, Chris, and their two kids to Las Vegas to get away for the weekend. During the trip, we took the grandkids to The Adventure Dome, and to my surprise, most of the rides are still there, and they still have the same names.

In the amusement park world, that's a lifetime.

The lesson? When you have a creative challenge, if it's possible, go to the source. See the actual location, and if possible, find the audience you need to reach and get its advice. Through focus groups, surveys, research trips, and even casual conversation, you'll often hit the target much more accurately—especially when you include stakeholders or anyone who will interact or benefit from the project. I'm not a research expert, but I'll take any information I can get that helps me get inside the mind of the audience I'm trying to target.

On a recent project with a television station, we did phone and online surveys with viewers, and that information was invaluable for helping us understand their viewing habits. Even when the client won't pay for it, I'll often do my own man-on-the-street interviews, informal online surveys, or personal calls.

As creative people, we often assume we can come up with anything. But why go through that pressure when the answers might already be in front of us?

Oh, and one more thing: Don't tell Circus Circus that The Adventure Dome rides were named by my daughter's second grade class in Burbank, California.

I never mentioned that in my presentation.

CHAPTER 16

SHOWERS, DRIVING, AND THE THINKING CHAIR

The relaxing, solitary, and non-judgmental shower environment may afford creative thinking by allowing the mind to wander freely, and causing people to be more open to their inner stream of consciousness and daydreams.

—Scott Barry Kaufman, cognitive scientist

As weird as it may sound, one of the best places for me to get ideas is in the shower. I can't explain it, but once the water starts, the ideas flow. Some researchers attribute it to our relaxed state, others to released dopamine in the brain, and still others to the distraction of the shower itself.

Whatever it is, it works. Scott Barry Kaufman, a cognitive scientist and co-author of *Wired to Create*, described a study he did showing that 72 percent of people get creative ideas in the shower, so apparently, I'm in good company. Kaufman also reported that his research reveals that more people have creative moments in the shower than at work. His thesis is the distraction factor—we're isolated from people, phone calls, emails, and other distractions, so our minds can be fully relaxed.

The website Mental Floss confirms that idea:

Since these routines don't require much thought, you flip to autopilot. This frees up your unconscious to work on something else. Your mind goes wandering, leaving your brain to quietly play a no-holds-barred game of free association.

So the next time you're up against the wall, take a shower! I've known all kinds of creative people who had showers installed in their offices just for generating ideas. Don't be afraid to head to the bathroom and turn on the water.

For a long time, my problem with showers was that by the time I'd get out, dry off, and find a pen and paper, I'd forgotten most of those creative insights. I was complaining about that one day in our office when someone suggested Aqua Notes—a waterproof notepad that comes with suction cups to easily mount on the shower tile.

It was a miracle. Now I can write down anything that comes.

I may stay in the shower for the rest of my life.

TAKE A DRIVE

I have so many ideas while driving, it makes my wife, Kathleen, nuts. I don't want to have a wreck, so I'm constantly asking her to grab my phone or notepad and jot down another idea that's popped into my head. I have to agree with music legend Willie Nelson: "When I'm driving the highway by myself is when I write best."

Similar to what happens in the shower, while driving, the conscious mind is paying attention to the road, and the unconscious mind is free to wander, so that's when ideas often happen. However, it doesn't work (for most people) if you're listening to an audiobook or podcast. In those cases, you're getting caught up in the conversation or story, and your mind is focused on the narrative and not as free to make random connections.

And the not-so-surprising news is that sitting alone with our thoughts is a real challenge. In a recent study led by Professor Timothy Wilson at the University of Virginia and published in the journal *Science*, a group of college students were asked if they would be able to sit quietly for fifteen minutes or if they preferred an electric shock. To the researcher's surprise, simply being alone with their own thoughts for fifteen minutes was apparently so challenging that 67 percent of the males and 25 percent of the females chose to have the electric shock and be done with it.

But if you can bring yourself to the point of unplugging, try it the next time you're in the car. Turn off the music, podcast, or audiobook. Focus consciously on the road, and see what comes to your mind—especially if you're facing a creative challenge.

THE THINKING CHAIR

Leadership expert and coach John Maxwell has written many great books including, *The 21 Irrefutable Laws of Leadership* and *The 21 Indispensable Qualities of a Leader*. His books have sold millions of copies, with some on the *New York Times* best-seller list, and he's taught a generation of leaders how to be more effective in their roles. I've had the opportunity to share the stage with John at a few conferences over the years, and I've been particularly fascinated with the idea of his "thinking chair."

As John tells it, he keeps a chair in his office that he only uses for thinking. He doesn't write, do research, make calls, or anything else in that chair.

He just thinks.

It echoes the stories of many writers who value a routine. There's something in our subconscious that a regular routine turns into a habit. When I show up at my writing desk day after day, it sends a signal to my brain that it's time to write.

In a similar way, doctors will often tell patients with insomnia to stop doing anything else in their beds other than sleeping. Don't read books, watch TV, or eat a meal. Doing all those other tasks confuses the brain about the purpose of the bed, which eventually can result in insomnia. But when you only use your bed for sleeping, it doesn't take long for your brain to associate "bed" with "time to sleep."

I'm not sure what they say about sex, but back to our subject. . . .

John's thinking chair has trained his mind to spring into action when he sits down. By only using that particular chair for thinking, something gets switched on deep in his brain that causes the ideas to flow.

So many ideas flow, in fact, that John is in demand from Fortune 500 companies, international government leaders, and organizations as diverse as the NFL and the U.S. Military Academy at West Point. Three of his books have sold more than a million copies, and he was one of twenty-five authors named to Amazon.com's 10th Anniversary Hall of Fame.

Apparently, his thinking chair works.

The important thing is to experiment and find the places or actions that inspire creativity for you.

Famed ballet choreographer George Balanchine found that place doing his laundry. He once said, "When I'm ironing, that's when I do most of my work."

In a more bizarre idea, inventor Yoshiro Nakamatsu, who invented the floppy disk and has at least three thousand patents, believes the closer to death he can get, the more creative he becomes. His preferred method is free diving underwater. He attempts to stay under until a flash of inspiration happens—which sometimes could be seconds before drowning.

I love swimming, but not quite that much.

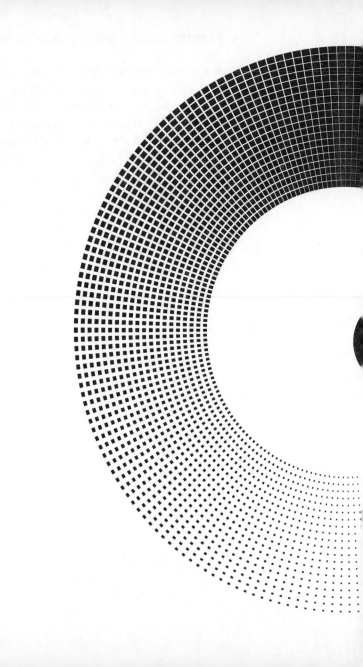

CHAPTER 17

THE POWER OF A GOOD WALK

Everywhere is within walking distance if you have the time.

—Steven Wright, comedian

There have been libraries written about how often walking is the best tool for generating ideas as far back as Aristotle. This famous Greek philosopher actually did his teaching while walking around his school in Athens. His students literally followed him around, giving rise to the term peripatetic philosophers—which is a Greek word for walking about (actually meandering).

In London a few years ago, I picked up a marvelous little book by Charles Dickens called *Night Walks*, where he details his period as an insomniac and decided the cure was to take long walks throughout London in the middle of the night. His reports of the homelessness, drunkenness, vice, and violence on the streets during those hours is a fascinating read.

Dickens had always been a walker and twenty- to-thirty-mile hikes were pretty normal. It's been reported that he walked so much, his friends became worried that he might have a mental problem. But over his career, those walks inspired him to write more than a dozen classic novels, several short story collections, nonfiction books, and even a few plays. Many of his most memorable characters were likely the result of people he observed on those walks.

I'm also a great fan of Danish theologian and writer Soren Kierkegaard. As you read the great body of Kierkegaard's writing, it's pretty clear that walking and writing were the most important pursuits in his life. Living in Copenhagen, he would write until about noon, then take a long walk, pondering that morning's work. Then it was back for more writing. He said:

> Above all, do not lose your desire to walk. Every day, I walk myself into a state of well-being & walk away from every illness. I have walked myself into my best thoughts, and I know of no thought so burdensome that one cannot walk away from it. But by sitting still, & the more one sits still, the closer one comes to feeling ill. Thus if one just keeps on walking, everything will be all right.

Every type of creative endeavor has an advocate of walking. From composer Ludwig van Beethoven to naturalist and conservationist John Muir, physicist Albert Einstein, and Apple's Steve Jobs—all shared a common joy of walking.

> *I can only meditate when I am walking. When I stop,*
> *I cease to think, my mind only works with my legs.*
> —JEAN-JACQUES ROUSSEAU, *Confessions*

Today, what those great thinkers advocated is being supported by more and more research. One study of radiologists revealed that they were more likely to identify potential problems on patient x-rays if they examined them while walking rather than sitting in an office.

In 2014, the American Psychological Association published a study from Marily Oppezzo and colleague Daniel L. Schwartz, PhD, from Stanford University, called, "Give Your Ideas Some Legs: The Positive Effect of Walking on Creative Thinking." Oppezzo reported in a press release:

> *Asking someone to take a 30-minute run to improve creativity at work would be an unpopular prescription for many people. We wanted to see if a simple walk might lead to more free-flowing thoughts and more creativity. Participants came up with fewer novel ideas when they sat for the second test set after walking during the first. However, they did perform better than the participants who sat for both sets of tests, so there was a residual effect of walking on creativity when people sat down afterward. Walking before a meeting that requires innovation may still be nearly as useful as walking during the meeting.*

In another test, they discovered students doubled the number of novel responses when walking than when sitting. And lest you think it's just the fact of being outdoors, she responded, "While being outdoors has many cognitive benefits, walking appears to have a very specific benefit of improving creativity."

The *New York Times* reported on the study:

> *For almost every student, creativity increased substantially when they walked. Most were able to generate about 60 percent more uses for an object, and the ideas were both novel and appropriate.*

> **Vasari wrote in 1550 that when Renaissance painter Paolo Uccello was working out the laws of visual perspective, he would walk back and forth all night, muttering to**

himself: "What a beautiful thing is this perspective!"
while his wife called him back to bed with no success.
—MIHALY CSIKSZENTMIHALYI, AUTHOR OF *FLOW:*
THE PSYCHOLOGY OF OPTIMAL EXPERIENCE

In my own case, my wife, Kathleen, and I live up against the Verdugo Mountains in Los Angeles and love hiking various trails near our home. I'm a morning person, so I focus on writing first thing and then spend many afternoons walking in the hills—particularly when I get stuck on a problem.

In my opinion, "getting stuck" is the greatest reason for walking. There's something about turning your focus elsewhere that makes ideas happen more easily. At the same time, any type of physical movement is better than nothing. There's something about physical activity that actually changes the way we think.

Working in the entertainment industry in Los Angeles has shown me the great number of actors who don't even start memorizing lines until the director starts blocking a scene. Apparently, it's the act of physical movement that helps them memorize their parts. Our daughter Kelsey and her husband, Chris Guerra, are both actors and producers and just released a feature "mockumentary" titled *Re-Opening*. Chris is also a member of the prestigious Groundlings Theater Company in Hollywood—famous for training some of the greatest comic actors of our time. Kelsey and Chris tell me that even with spontaneous improvisation, some of their best lines are triggered by moving from one place to another on the stage as opposed to sitting, standing, or doing some other physical action.

Even fidgeting can deliver positive results (which is good for me.) I bought a fitness watch to monitor my physical activity and was shocked to find out how many steps I take in a day without ever leaving my office. Even when I think I'm sitting at my desk all day working, my watch told me a different story. It made me realize that I'm constantly getting up to get another cup of coffee, go to the restroom, talk to a colleague, check on my wife—in short, most of us move far more than we think.

But while any activity is a positive thing, just puttering around the office won't reap a big harvest of creative ideas.

Not all physical activity helps.

For a time, I set up a basketball goal in my driveway, and when I would get creatively stuck, I'd go out and shoot some baskets. It helped, but I eventually realized I was concentrating so much on my shooting that I wasn't experiencing many breakthroughs.

Then I hung a heavy boxing bag in the garage, and while punching it helped me get rid of my frustrations, it wasn't putting me in a creative mindset either.

Running is similar. There's something about speed that keeps me from finding a state where I can reflect on creative challenges, but I admit that for others it may be different. Acclaimed novelist Haruki Murakami is a regular runner and even wrote the book, *What I Talk About When I Talk About Running.* Joyce Carol Oates, Malcolm Gladwell, and others are committed runners, but in my experience running is more like my sessions with the boxing bag. It's not for reflection; it's for exhaustion.

And that's when I discovered walking.

> *I have walked myself into the best thoughts.*
> —Soren Kierkegaard, theologian and philosopher

As I walk, I'm not really concentrating on anything. While I'm observing the world around me, there's no real skill involved, and I'm not trying to improve my ability as a walker, I just walk. That frees up my mind to be more receptive to random associations and whatever idea pops into my head.

And for the record, numerous studies indicate that walking in nature may be more creatively productive than walking in the city. Aside from the quiet, nature is visually "softer" and not as detailed.

On my visits to New York City, I walk for miles, but I find myself noticing specific things around me. The homeless man on the sidewalk, the police officer directing traffic, architectural features of a building, a jacket in a shop window, watching the crowds, and more. The more detail I notice, the less I think and reflect and the less chance of a creative breakthrough.

As I mentioned earlier, although I live in Los Angeles, my home is a block from the Verdugo Mountains, so when I walk, it doesn't feel like an urban setting. But when I visit another city like New York, London, or Chicago, I spend more time noticing things that are new to me.

However, if you live in an urban environment and are familiar with the local surroundings, you may not be distracted as much as I am, so walking in the city might work for you just as it did for Charles Dickens.

Either way, random and unexpected connections are the key, and when walking, you have to free your mind to be open when they arrive. I have friends who start walking but begin thinking about an old love affair, a problem employee at work, or a family issue. They get so caught up in that particular mindset, they shut off the very thing that walking helps with—being open to unexpected connections. Certainly we can't walk with a completely clean slate, but do your best to not get bogged down focusing on one issue—especially if it's negative or frustrating.

I'll often run through the problem that has me stuck and then push it aside to watch a deer on the mountain or a snake cross the road. Sometimes, I'll stop at the overlook and look out over the San Fernando Valley.

It's during those random moments that the breakthrough often happens.

*Methinks that the moment my legs begin
to move, my thoughts begin to flow.*
—HENRY DAVID THOREAU, AUTHOR

When I joined a local gym, the manager told me the vast majority of members come in to exercise after work. But after learning how many creative and productive benefits physical exercise and movement can bring, it might be worth rethinking our workout schedules. Perhaps we could start the day with a workout, or better yet, break up the day into "mini-workouts" that involve walking, exercise, or whatever works for you.

Everyone is different and lives in different locations, so your walking space may be an urban area downtown, suburbia, a beach, or a dirt road. Whatever it is, do your best to find a place that you enjoy and start today.

And if you'd like to explore the benefits of walking, I'd encourage you to check out books like:

In Praise of Walking: A New Scientific Exploration, by Shane O'Mara
Wanderlust: A History of Walking, by Rebecca Solnit
From Here To There: The Art and Science of Losing Our Way, by Michael Bond

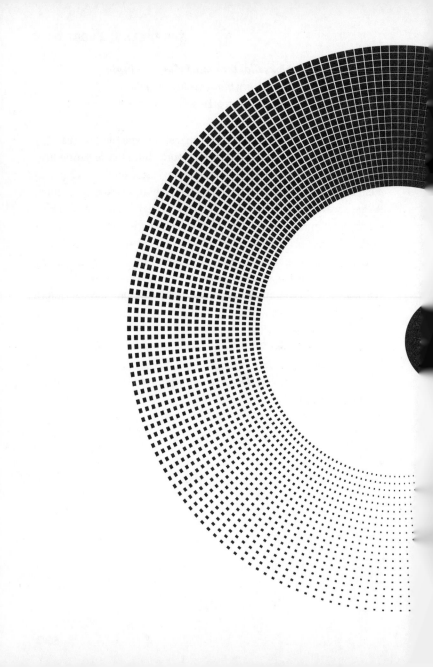

CHAPTER 18

THE HOLY TRINITY OF CREATIVITY:

FIND THE PLACE, SCHEDULE THE TIME, AND SHOW UP

Routine, in an intelligent man, is a sign of ambition. . . .
A modern stoic knows that the surest way to discipline
passion is to discipline time: decide what you want or ought
to do during the day, then always do it at exactly the same
moment every day, and passion will give you no trouble.

–W. H. Auden, poet

Over the years, I've written while on a freighter traveling up the Amazon River, during a military coup in Africa, and sitting in a nomadic tent in Mongolia when it was minus sixteen degrees outside and snowing. I've been locked up in thousands of hotel rooms, worked on as many airline flights, and had a terrific idea sitting in the heat outside an Egyptian pyramid. War correspondents have written news stories with bullets flying by their heads, and while novelist Ernest Hemingway was recovering from his war wounds in an Italian hospital, he wrote stories on Red Cross stationery.

Creative people will work in whatever place they find themselves. But for me, there's one place that's my favorite place in the world for ideas—*my desk in my home office*. And the best time for me to be there? In the morning, preferably between 6:00 a.m. and noon.

You'll never become a first-class creative professional until you can generate great ideas nearly anywhere or anytime—much like me in that TV producer's conference room scared half to death. But what keeps that engine running is regularly showing up at the same place and time.

WHAT'S YOUR PLACE?

My "go-to" creative place is my home office because I've customized it for everything I need. My library, references, tech gadgets, computer plugs and connectors, big monitor, and more (like my rocking chair, for instance) are all there, so I have everything at my fingertips. After doing it almost on a daily basis for so many years, it's almost like a switch is flipped when the seat of my pants comes in contact with the seat of my chair.

The creative part of my brain turns on.

I always encourage young creatives to find a similar place that contains everything they need to do the job and where they are comfortable and have privacy. The importance of location can't be overstated because great athletes will always tell you there's a serious advantage competing in their home stadium.

Obviously, if you have roommates or kids, it's more of a challenge to find that favorite quiet place. Many creative people work before the kids are up or after they go to bed. But your spot doesn't even have to be at home. It could be a local library (after all, no one else uses them anymore), a coffee shop, or the office when others aren't working. Wherever it is, you need to make it routine. Show up on a regular basis.

When his kids were small, Todd Komarnicki, producer of *Elf*, writer of *Sully: The Untold Story Behind the Miracle on the Hudson*, and as of this writing, the writer/producer of a new Netflix dramatic series, lived in a New York City apartment. To get the peace and quiet he needed for writing each day, he would make the rounds of multiple restaurants in his neighborhood. He'd start writing at a local coffee shop early in the morning; then, by noon, he'd move to a diner. In the afternoon, he'd end up working at the corner seat at a local pub. The staff at each location knew him because he was a regular, and he treated it the same as going into a normal office.

The point is, whatever works for you is fine, as long as you stick to it.

I was thinking about this a few years ago while my wife, Kathleen, and I toured the Charles Dickens Museum in London. His main study was built around his writing desk, and he understood the importance of finding the right place and sticking to a schedule. An overwhelming number of creative people (particularly writers) have done the same thing:

- Ernest Hemingway wrote at a stand-up table.
- Truman Capote wrote lying down.
- Jane Austen wrote in her parlor, at a small table barely large enough to hold the papers she was writing on.
- Toni Morrison writes at a hotel.
- Cervantes, Bunyan, and the apostle Paul wrote in prison (not necessarily a preference).
- Annie Dillard prefers a room with no view.
- Agatha Christie liked to write in the desert where there weren't any distractions.

I could go on and on, but the point is this:

Great creative people must discover the space where they can focus and be most productive.

Where's that place for you?

Human beings are simply wired for a regular routine and once you tap into that, everything changes.

Everyone is different, and different people need different environments to flourish. For me, I have an incredibly high distraction factor, so I need to be someplace where I won't be interrupted. It's serious enough that inside a bank vault might be the best location for me to generate ideas. For instance, in my home office, I have five windows. As I mentioned earlier, three are translucent, so they let in light but I can't see what's outside, and the other two have shutters the size of two-by-fours. When I'm in my office, I'm in a bubble, and that's exactly the way I like it.

On the other hand, I know brilliant creative thinkers who love to work in a noisy and sometimes even chaotic atmosphere. They love open office plans and like to constantly bounce ideas off others, so the more, the merrier. You often find that kind of atmosphere in writing rooms for a network TV series. Typical episodic dramas are written by a team of writers who spend significant parts of their day developing concepts, arguing about ideas, and brainstorming around conference tables.

A great example of this is the documentary film *Get Back* directed by Peter Jackson. Created from sixty hours of film footage shot in 1969, it's a remarkable inside look at the creative style of how The Beatles worked. They rented a film studio, sat in a circle, and just made it up as they went. Out of that creative approach came some of their most memorable songs.

Whatever your job or career choice, if that helps generate ideas for you, then by all means gravitate toward the noise.

I've even seen research that indicates some creative people thrive in the dull roar of coffee shop conversation, which is probably why we see so many laptops open when we pick up our espresso.

The key issue is deciding what's really most productive for you.

Very often, when we hit a creative wall, we seek out other ideas and gravitate toward coworkers, friends, and others who are willing to kick around ideas until we feel like something hits. There's companionship in misery, and we hope against hope that other voices or spending a little time on social media will inspire us to think differently.

However, just as often, that's simply distracting yourself from the hard work of creating, and for me, that work takes place by myself.

The critical thing is to find that place. By the time you finish this book, my goal is to inspire your confidence to be able to produce great ideas anywhere, anytime. But batteries must be recharged, and what gives us the skill and energy to create those ideas in unusual places is the history and track record of creating in the location that we love.

SCHEDULE THE TIME

The second issue to face is determining what time of day you are most creative. This isn't the place to go into the science of circadian rhythm, but I would encourage you to explore it further. What we call circadian rhythm or cycles is essentially an internal clock that regulates our sleeping and waking cycles every twenty-four hours. It's essentially the processes happening within our body as we respond to night and day, sleeping and waking, and it's also been observed in plants, animals, and some bacteria.

What circadian rhythm reveals is that there are certain times of the day when we're predisposed to be at our best. For instance, generally speaking, our lowest body temperature happens around 4:30 a.m., our sharpest rise in blood pressure is at 6:45 a.m., our alertness is high at 10:00 a.m., our best physical coordination happens around 2:00 p.m., and our greatest muscle strength comes around 5:00 p.m.

There are far more physical indicators during a typical twenty-four-hour period, and while we don't all share the same clock, it's important (I would say critical) to discover your clock and respect it.

When it comes to creativity, I join a significant part of the creative community that rocks roughly between 6:00 a.m. and noon. After lunch, I'm good for meetings, phone calls, responding to email, traveling, and more, but when it comes to creativity, I don't rise to the occasion nearly as well as I do in the morning. When I wake up, the birds are chirping, a heavenly choir is singing, and I'm ready to take on the world.

My wife, Kathleen? Not so much.

Kathleen is in another large creative group that keeps rockstar hours. She's much slower than I am to get out of bed, and she prefers to work later in the day and into the evening. Often, at the end of a long day when I'm barely functioning, she's at her peak performance. Needless to say, that can add some challenging wrinkles to a marriage, but after so many years of give-and-take, we've worked it out and actually thrive with the difference.

There's also a creative group that hits their stride in the afternoon. That couldn't be any more different than me, but I'm grateful *somebody* is at their best when I'm at my worst.

Just like finding your ultimate creative location, you need to find your best time of day and protect it as your creative time.

Obviously, many reading this will have a day job and can't work on their novel, new design, marketing plan, or other ideas during the workday. But once you discover your peak time, you can start to better adjust your day around your creative peaks.

For instance, after struggling for years to write my first book, I discovered I was a morning person. At the time, I was working full-time on a television series, but I started coming in two hours before anyone else to work on my manuscript. It was quiet, no phones were ringing, and I had no distractions. As a result, I wrote my first two books by coming in a couple of hours early for work every day and maximizing my most productive hours.

Whether you're full-time or self-employed, how could you adjust your day in a way that would begin to honor your best creative moments? Find it, and as much as humanly possible, build a protective wall around those hours. As you develop your best location and time of day into your daily schedule, it will become a routine, and any experienced creative professional will tell you that's the starting point to reaching your creative potential.

SHOW UP

The final third of the holy trinity of creativity is simply showing up. Professional creatives don't wait for the idea to come to them; they go after the idea. Novelist Jack London famously said, "You can't wait for inspiration. You have to go after it with a club."

When it comes to generating great ideas, we've already discussed that feelings can't be in charge. Feelings come and go and will almost always lead you in the wrong direction when it comes to original thinking. Add the emotional pressure of delivering on a deadline, and things get worse. But time and again, the greatest thinkers have discovered that *action breeds feelings more effectively than feelings lead to action*. Which means stop waiting 'til you feel like it. Just start, and the feeling will come.

IDEAS ON A DEADLINE

In 1911, writer and activist Mary Heaton Vorse encouraged young novelist Sinclair Lewis: "The art of writing is connecting the seat of your pants to the seat of a chair." Apparently he listened, and eventually became the first American to win the Nobel Prize in literature.

If you wanted to make real progress with physical training, you wouldn't think of working out just once a week. Commitment is the key to generating ideas, and it takes a regular schedule for your mind to get the concept. When you show up day after day at the same place and time, your mind starts to get the picture and kicks into gear.

This is probably why when playwright, novelist, and short-story writer Somerset Maugham was asked if he wrote when he was inspired or on a daily schedule, he replied: "I write only when inspiration strikes. Fortunately it strikes every morning at nine o'clock sharp."

Show up and the ideas will come.

To go deeper into creative routines, I would encourage you to read Mason Currey's book *Daily Rituals: How Artists Work*. It's a brilliant survey of some of the most famous filmmakers, artists, writers, poets, scientists, and other creative professionals and their personal routines and rituals. Once you read how this collection of 161 inspiring minds developed daily creative habits, you'll never look at your schedule the same way again.

CHAPTER 19

HOLD BACK THE FLOOD

Call me irresponsible, but I always wait until the traffic man appears at the door, purple faced and screaming for my copy. <u>Then</u> I write it. I find there is a direct correlation between rising panic and burgeoning inspiration.

—**Adrian Holmes, award-winning advertising copywriter**

When it comes to creative ideas, early in my career, I learned the value of waiting as long as possible. For instance, when I start a script, blog post, article, or book, the last thing I do is to actually write. Even when I feel the thoughts coming together, I fight the urge to sit down. Despite the schedule or approaching deadline, I let it churn around inside, bang about in my head, and percolate, and only when I can't hold back any longer, I fire up the laptop and start writing.

I often joke that I don't even think about starting a project until I see the deadline looming in the distance. Earlier, I described it as the adrenaline rush a pilot feels during liftoff when he sees the end of the runway coming closer and closer.

Whatever it is, seeing that deadline gets my heart pumping and my blood flowing. When that happens, a flood of creative ideas start, and it's sometimes difficult to type fast enough to keep up.

I'm a firm believer that a significant number of creative people who suffer from writer's block are simply starting their projects too soon. They may have the initial concept of the project in mind, but the ideas come at a trickle. But when you dam up the river, the level builds and builds so that when you open the floodgate, the torrent begins.

> *I spend a lot of time fact-finding, and I don't start writing until I have too much to say. I don't believe you can write fluent copy if you have to interrupt yourself with research. Dig first, then write.*
> —David Abbott, advertising copywriter and member of The One Show Hall of Fame

So, start by not starting. Do your research, collect books and articles on the topic, and if there's a location, visit it. Reflect. Think. Ponder.

But be careful about talking about it. When you're in the process of a particular project, talking about your creative challenge—even to other creative people—is like sneaking open one of the floodgates just a bit. It doesn't do much good and, in fact, lets the momentum eventually trickle out.

> *Let the pressure build.*
> —Ernest Hemingway, novelist and Nobel Prize winner

Early in our marriage, I took my wife, Kathleen, on a surprise hot-air balloon trip for her birthday. We woke up before sunrise and drove about an hour or two out of town to an empty field where the balloon and basket were both ready. I had my doubts about the pilot, but we had an incredible morning flying over fields, lakes, and more than a few farmhouses.

A couple of hours into the trip, the pilot noticed an air leak in the balloon. It wasn't an immediate emergency, but we could see that we were slowly losing pressure and altitude as well. The pilot skillfully fired up the heater to keep us going, but eventually we needed to land—long before our intended destination.

We were on the outskirts of a small rural town when we were finally forced down into the backyard of a shocked family who was having breakfast. By then, the air was leaking pretty quickly, and we hit hard, were ejected from the basket, and took a tumble.

For me, that's pretty much what talking about a creative project before its time is like. It doesn't help, it deflates my momentum, and eventually the entire idea fizzles.

BRAINSTORMING RARELY WORKS

In my experience, brainstorming rarely works. There's no question that brainstorming is popular—very popular—especially in corporations and nonprofit organizations. But the truth is, research has shown over and over that people produce better quality ideas when they start by working alone. Yet, many advertising agencies, companies, and nonprofits have enshrined "brainstorming" as the number one go-to method for coming up with new ideas.

Creativity is obviously tough, so many think if you can get lots of people in a room, the pressure on individuals is off. In other words, the people who should be coming up with the breakthrough ideas pass it off to "group think" and duck the difficult work of developing original and creative thinking.

Another reason is that a cardinal brainstorming rule is there's no place for criticism during a session. The idea is that when you criticize someone for an idea you don't like, you may hurt their feelings, and they'll clam up. Worse, perhaps their next idea would have been the big one, but now your criticism has shut them down.

That may be true in some situations—especially with young or inexperienced people. But it's also worth noting that if you're working with people who get their feelings hurt when you take a hard look at their ideas, then you're working with amateurs. Creative professionals aren't sissies—they understand that ideas should be vetted and, yes,—criticized—before they go to market. Don't be a jerk about it, and don't talk down to people, but if you're working with people whose feelings get hurt every time their ideas are seriously discussed, then they probably shouldn't even be in the room.

Here's my recommendation: *Start Alone.*

If you're a creative professional, then shut the door, and get to work. If you're a leader, then give everyone on the team the individual task of developing the first stages of the idea. Only after they actually have something, bring them in the room together to discuss, debate, and even (dare I say) criticize the ideas.

The critical key is to come together *only after they have something*. This means if they aren't willing to do the hard work of starting with a blank page and actually developing rough ideas, then they shouldn't be allowed in the room. A group can hone, craft, and develop the ideas, but time after time, you'll find the best ideas start with a single person.

And it's worth noting that getting more people in the room doesn't help coming up with original ideas.

I love being around creative people. I love getting their advice and counsel. But ultimately, if I'm looking for a game-changing idea, long experience has taught me that it's time to close the door and start with a blank page. I know I'll get some haters for that message, but the reasons brainstorming by committee rarely works are many:

1) Research indicates that a number of individuals working alone will generate more diverse and better-quality ideas than the same number participating in a brainstorming session.

2) When you have too many people commenting on creative work, it gets reduced to the lowest level possible. By its very nature, we can't do breakthrough work if we have to please everyone. Throw up a Google doc and ask everyone to comment, and everyone will—whether they have good ideas or not. Everyone wants to participate and look involved, so they can't help themselves.

3) Theoretically, we're not supposed to judge ideas during a brainstorming session, but even when others don't, we judge our own. After all, most of the best ideas sound ridiculous or crazy at first, and who wants to look crazy in front of the team? As a result, self-censorship happens, and the best ideas can be held back.

4) Introverts often get left out. Studies have shown that in most brainstorming sessions, the people with dominant, outgoing personalities get most of the attention. They're assertive. They get excited. As a result, the introverts (who may be the smartest people in the room) back down or stay quiet.

5) Everyone generates ideas at different speeds. Some people are good at spouting off the first thing that pops into their head, while others need more time. Personally, I can't stand to be in a room where people are shouting suggestions because it's just too distracting. I need quiet and some time to let my thinking develop.

6) Brainstorming is usually championed by the least creative person on the team. He or she may be a leader or team member, but they know they need others to raise their profile because they're not coming up with ideas on their own. They believe a group will help.

> *Few things in life are less efficient than a group of*
> *people trying to write a sentence. The advantage*
> *of this method is that you end up with something*
> *for which you will not be personally blamed.*
> —SCOTT ADAMS, CREATOR OF *DILBERT*

If you're a leader, consider cutting back the number of creative meetings and brainstorming sessions with your entire team, and if you're not the leader, be skeptical and avoid as many as you possibly can. While it may seem obvious that a group of people is always better than one, study after study says otherwise. Organizations continue hosting brainstorming sessions, filling up conference rooms with people, poster boards, and sticky notes, even though more and more research says it's simply not as effective as many believe.

Sessions like this may generate more ideas, but it's time you started a shift to generating better ideas.

Make the decision of who the creative person is that you want in charge and accountable for the project, and let them run. You'll be glad you did.

> *"There is in my heart as it were a burning fire shut up in*
> *my bones, and I am weary of holding it in, and I cannot."*
> —JEREMIAH 20:9 (ESV)

The next step is to let it all out. The secret to getting great ideas is, at the right moment, get it all out. When I get to the point that I can't hold it in anymore, I open the floodgates because I want everything on the table.

On that first pass, I edit very little and don't worry much about accuracy, grammar, the project's budget, timetable, or anything else.

I worry about getting everything down.

As a result, in most cases I over-create. With one book, I literally wrote enough for two complete books before I started editing it down into something that actually worked. Anything that pops into my head, anything from my research and notes—whatever—I want to get it down because you never know how it will all interact later.

D. H. Lawrence rewrote his entire novel *Lady Chatterley's Lover* three times before he considered it finished. Ernest Hemingway said, "I wrote the ending to *Farewell to Arms*, the last page of it, thirty-nine times before I was satisfied."

Working this way probably makes me more of a rewriter than a writer. Even Tolstoy, the genius behind the epic novel *War and Peace*, wrote:

I don't know how anyone can write without rewriting everything over and over again. I scarcely ever re-read my published writings, but if by chance I come across a page, it always strikes me: All this must be rewritten; this is how I should have written it.

THE CURE FOR WRITER'S BLOCK?

For me, the act of spilling my guts is also a cure for writer's block because, in that initial phase of the project, there's no pressure. I'm not trying to shape the final project or have a breakthrough moment, so I can jot down anything that comes to mind. I'll worry about editing later, so at this first stage, anything can happen.

With that pressure out of the way, the ideas are more likely to start flowing. It doesn't have to be pretty because you're not showing this to anyone, so just let it go.

CHAPTER 20

YOUR CRISIS MAY BE THE KEY TO YOUR CREATIVITY

Sometimes you need a little crisis to get your adrenaline flowing and help you realize your potential.

—Jeannette Walls, *The Glass Castle*

When it comes to being creative under pressure, when the clock starts ticking and you have a hard delivery date, there's no pressure like a crisis. The most urgent creative challenges don't happen under arbitrary deadlines or normal schedules—they happen because there is no other way out.

- When your advertising campaign is the last chance to save the product.
- When you have to present to the board a reorganization plan.
- When your speech needs to turn the tide for a political candidate.
- When your fundraising effort must save the nonprofit.
- When you have to face the public after a company scandal.

I could go on and on, but know that as a creative professional, there will be plenty of times when you won't get a second chance. When more is on the line than the possibility of criticism. When all that stands between success and failure is your idea.

One of my favorite lines in film is when Orson Welles improvised a scene while playing Harry Lime in *The Third Man* in 1949:

> *"In Italy, for thirty years under the Borgias, they had warfare, terror, murder, and bloodshed, but they produced Michelangelo, Leonardo da Vinci, and the Renaissance. In Switzerland, they had brotherly love, they had five hundred years of democracy and peace—and what did that produce? The cuckoo clock."*

As creatives, we work hard trying to create a perfect world in which to work. We want all the best tools and resources, the right team around us, and leaders who understand us. We want people to be nice and supportive. Most of all, we want plenty of time.

But the truth is, when you look at the pantheon of artistic work throughout the centuries, the greatest creativity was often expressed in the midst of war, economic uncertainty, fear, or through the haze of addiction, mental illness, or abuse. Sometimes, it's having to work under an incompetent, nasty, brutish boss.

Sure, great work has sometimes been done by rich people in cushy circumstances or by normal people having a nice life. But when you compare that to the massive amount of creative work born from poverty, pain, frustration, abuse, and repression, it doesn't really balance.

For a creative person, the difficult circumstances you're going through right now may be the greatest gift you've ever received.

Work to make things better. Rise up. Do what you can to relieve the pain. But the truth is, pain is often the foundry where great creative work is formed.

I know in my own life, looking back, times of fear, uncertainty, pain, or working for a raging jerk were also electric with possibilities. I was forced to express myself because there was no alternative. Creating with no safety net can be terrifying and exhilarating all at the same time.

In 1777, Samuel Johnson said, "Depend upon it, sir, when a man knows he is to be hanged in a fortnight, it concentrates his mind wonderfully." When all the other options are gone, your creative horizon becomes very clear.

Today, stop complaining, and start creating. Don't *celebrate* the obstacles, but *embrace* them. Realize that you stand in a long line of creative men and women who broke through the barriers—no matter how great—and created something for the ages.

I've heard every excuse under the sun that keeps people from creating great work. "I'm too busy and can't find the time," ranks right at the top, along with whining, "I get distracted," or "I'm tired after working at my day job." But remember the challenges Spanish novelist Miguel de Cervantes experienced, and suddenly, our feeble excuses don't sound like much. Here's the way writer David Wootton described it:

> *This year marks the 400th anniversary of the death of Miguel de Cervantes, the author of* Don Quixote *(1605). Cervantes had fought and been badly injured at the 1571 battle of Lepanto; later he was captured by Barbary pirates and held as a slave by the Ottomans for five years while awaiting ransom. He made*

repeated attempts to escape in full knowledge of the gruesome
fate that awaited him the moment his captors decided he was
more trouble than he was worth: A slave who helped him in
one of his attempts was tortured to death before his eyes. Free
at last, he became a playwright and tax collector and spent
time in prison for debt. It was in prison that he began his great
work. Although Don Quixote was an immediate and extraor-
dinary success, Cervantes made (in the absence of any form of
copyright) little from it and died in poverty. Don Quixote is
indisputably one of the greatest novels of all time.

More and more studies confirm that a crisis actually boosts creativity.
Remember that whatever crisis you're experiencing could be the forge
that fires your greatest creativity. So until we get wounded in battle,
held as a slave, or imprisoned (or all of the above), we should all shut
up and get back to work.

It's easy to see why we all live in a state of constant frustration. CNN
reports that we consume about seventy-four gigabytes—nine DVDs
worth—of data every day. And that overwhelming barrage of information doesn't include personal problems, career challenges, and other
obstacles. But the *Wall Street Journal* confirms that "having your world
turned upside down sparks creative thinking." How?

The journal puts it in the context of why so many immigrants like
Victor Hugo, W. H. Auden, Vladimir Nabokov, Nikolas Tesla, Marie
Curie, Sigmund Freud, and Albert Einstein have shown extraordinary
signs of genius:

Several studies have shed light on the role of "schema violations"
in intellectual development. A schema violation occurs when
our world is turned upside-down, when temporal and spatial
cues are off-kilter. In a 2011 study led by the Dutch psychologist
Simone Ritter and published in the Journal of Experimental
Social Psychology, *researchers asked some subjects to make*
breakfast in the "wrong" order and others to perform the task

*in the conventional manner. Those in the first group—the ones
engaged in a schema violation—consistently demonstrated more
"cognitive flexibility," a prerequisite for creative thinking.*

This suggests that it isn't the immigrants' ambition or even talent that
fully explains their creativity but their *marginality*. Many immigrants
possess what the psychologist Nigel Barber calls "oblique perspective."
Uprooted from the familiar, they see the world at an angle, and this fresh
perspective enables them to surpass the merely talented. To paraphrase
the philosopher Arthur Schopenhauer: "Talent hits a target no one else
can hit. Genius hits a target no one else can see."

In other words, having your world turned upside down can often
be the best spark for your creativity. That's not to say that getting fired,
experiencing a divorce, moving to another city, having a health setback,
or facing another crisis is a pleasant experience. But it does mean that
even the most difficult challenges we face can cause us to rethink how
we see the world and plant the seed of a new perspective.

During your next crisis, remember that it could be the key that could completely change your world for the better.

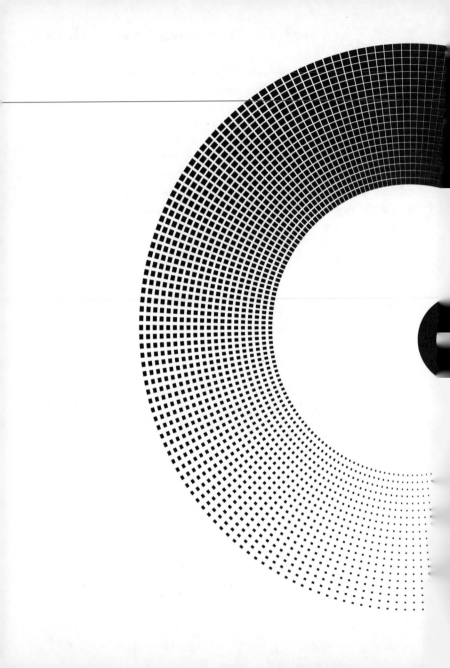

CHAPTER 21

THE POWER OF A "MASH-UP"

*Nothing is original. Steal from anywhere that resonates with
inspiration or fuels your imagination. Devour old films,
new films, music, books, paintings, photographs, poems,
dreams, random conversations, architecture, bridges, street
signs, trees, clouds, bodies of water, light and shadows.
Select only things to steal from that speak directly to your
soul. If you do this, your work (and theft) will be authentic.*

—Jim Jarmusch, film director and screenwriter

Hans Christian Andersen's ability to write fantastic and strange
fairy tales brought him worldwide fame in the nineteenth century. He wrote 156 stories published in nine volumes that have
been translated into more than 125 languages. His most famous fairy

tales include "The Emperor's New Clothes," "The Little Mermaid," "The Nightingale," "The Princess and the Pea," "The Snow Queen," "The Ugly Duckling," "The Little Match Girl," and "Thumbelina."

What most people don't realize is that he was inspired by wild tales he heard in a local asylum for the insane, where his grandmother worked as a gardener. He would go with her to work, and for hours, he would listen to the mental patients' crazy stories of witches, goblins, fairies, trolls, and more. Then he would take his notes, and with his writing gift, craft powerful stories that have fascinated readers for more than a century.

Andersen wasn't always original, but he was creative. He may have taken elements of his stories from psychiatric patients, but he created the ultimate finished work.

> *Good artists copy. Great artists steal.*
> —PABLO PICASSO, ARTIST

One big myth that holds creative people back is that they must be original in everything they do. As a result, they miss deadlines because they don't understand the power of a mash-up.

When George Lucas developed the idea for *Star Wars,* he was borrowing from the great storehouse of classic science fiction. Google didn't create the first search engine and was actually quite late to the game. What they did was design a far simpler interface which made it easier to use and then continued perfecting the results. In a similar way, Toshiba was manufacturing tablet devices for nearly ten years before Apple. Steve Jobs simply took the concept and perfected it.

> *What has been will be again, what has been done will*
> *be done again; there is nothing new under the sun.*
> —ECCLESIASTES 1:9 (NIV)

While we strive to be original in everything we do, the truth is that creative people are constantly borrowing from other sources. That doesn't mean they outright steal others' work. Plagiarism is flagrantly ripping someone off. That would be shameful and, in most cases, illegal.

But by studying the techniques, ideas, and results of other creative people, we can learn to see the world in a new way. Honestly, that's the essence of art: taking a bit from here, taking some from there, and combining them into something completely new.

That's why filmmakers like Martin Scorsese obsessively watch other directors' films. He wants to understand how other creative artists think and why they made those choices. Film director Jean-Luc Godard put it this way: "It's not where you take things from—it's where you take them to."

When it comes to advertising, I'm constantly watching TV commercials, print campaigns, and online design. I'm looking for new ideas and techniques—elements that I can integrate which will take my own work to a new level.

My office is filled with books on film and television production, writing, and creativity. As Michelangelo said, "I'm always learning," and to be at the top of our creative game, we need that same attitude.

COMBINING IDEAS FROM COMPLETELY DIFFERENT PLACES.

The story has been told many times, but one of the classic mash-up examples is from 1997 when Reed Hastings faced a $40 late fee for renting a videocassette of the movie *Apollo 13* from a Blockbuster video-rental store. He was so embarrassed he thought about not even mentioning it to his wife. But he paid the fee, and then drove to his workout for the day.

On the way to the gym, the thought occurred to him that, like his gym membership, *Why can't we pay a monthly fee and rent as many movies as we want? Why are we paying for each one and running up late fees when we can't get it back in time?*

The more he thought about it, the more he liked it, but that was back in the days of videocassettes, which were fragile and difficult to ship through the mail.

But he wouldn't let the idea go.

Soon, a friend tipped him off to a new technology—a digital video disk, or DVD. DVDs were smaller and flat, so they would be easier and less expensive to mail. He actually bought a handful of movies on DVD and then mailed them to himself. When they arrived undamaged, he knew his idea would work.

It was the mash-up of movies, his gym membership, and the kind of online retail business pioneered by companies like Amazon that made it work. He just needed to link those different ideas into one epic concept.

When he did that, Netflix was born.

The problem is, most of us stay stuck in one area, never considering how insight from other areas could join together to make a bigger idea.

> *Someone put a trolley and a suitcase together*
> *and got a suitcase with wheels.*
>
> *Someone put an igloo with a hotel and got an ice palace.*
>
> *Someone put a copier and a telephone*
> *together and got a fax machine.*
>
> *Someone put a bell and a clock together*
> *and got an alarm clock.*
>
> *Someone put a coin punch and a wine*
> *press together and we got books.*
> —PAUL SLOANE, *THE LEADER'S GUIDE*
> *TO LATERAL THINKING SKILLS*

SO WHEN YOU'RE UP AGAINST A DEADLINE:

First: Don't think your idea has to be something no one's ever thought of before. King Solomon, writing in Ecclesiastes nearly two hundred years before Christ knew that wasn't really possible. But what *can* be done is to learn from those who have gone before us, borrow elements, copy techniques, and use ideas that have worked in the past to create something entirely new.

Playwright George Bernard Shaw said: "Imitation is not just the sincerest form of flattery—it's the sincerest form of learning."

Second: Start mixing up ideas from different sources. The keys are being well-read, regularly talking to a wide range of people with different areas of expertise, and being open to different thinking and unusual solutions. Start being *intentional* about mixing what some might think are crazy ideas, and you never know where it might lead.

> *Since my early professional days, I have kept a file that is unnamed, unassuming, and filled with unusual and interesting clippings. Their only relationship to one another is that they captured my interest. They represent many design disciplines and mediums, yet fundamentally exhibit the same creative tools: shape, form, texture, scale, and color. They are my inspiration.*
> —BECKY BISHOP, LANDSCAPE ARCHITECT,
> WALT DISNEY IMAGINEERING

The late Steve Jobs said it best when he described his definition of creativity as exposing yourself "to the best things that humans have done" and then bringing "those things into what you are doing."

So get out there and start mashing things up!

163

CHAPTER 22

DREAMING AND CREATIVITY: DOES IT REALLY WORK?

If you have more inspiration in the middle of the night than you do in the middle of the day, then there's nothing to stop you from working when the rest of the people are sleeping. Get used to thinking out of the box if you want to be successful in your life.

—Lucas Bailly, *Happiness: Powerful Daily Habits To Be Happy, Stay Positive And Love Every Minute Of Your Life*

The idea that creative breakthroughs can happen during dreaming is as old as the ancient world. The Bible as well as other ancient writings are filled with references to men and women receiving divine messages during dreams, and written records of creative insights while we're asleep have continued right up to the present. The Victorian age experienced an explosion of serious scientific study of dreams, and before Sigmund Freud wrote his controversial *The Interpretation of Dreams*, there were explorations on the nature of dream symbols by writers like Karl Scherner in his 1861 book *Das Leben des Traumes* (The Life of Dreams).

The problem is, there is just as much scientific disagreement on the subject as there are reports of success.

Today, the subject of why we dream and the significance of our dreams is still hotly debated, and every year, it seems like more and more books are published on the subject. Current thinking is that dreaming could originate from a wide range of causes such as neurons firing in an effort to make subconscious sense of what we've recently experienced all the way to the theory that dreaming is the act of our mind sorting through memories of the recent past. Some believe it's like defragging a computer hard drive, rearranging our memories and eliminating the files we don't really need.

The theory that dreams are somehow sorting recent memories resonates most strongly with me. Just last night, my wife and I were watching a Spanish TV series closed-captioned in English. It was an over-the-top historical drama complete with medieval conspiracies within the king's court, clandestine affairs, and personal betrayals.

After watching last night's episode, I went to bed and began dreaming of my wife having an affair with an unknown but mysterious business partner of my daughter. Then I discovered my daughter spent $40,000 of my money (without my knowledge) to build some type of weird mechanical device to archive all of my books in our attic. She meant well, but I was so angry about her spending my money without my permission (not to mention my wife's affair) that I called an attorney and sued my daughter, started legal proceedings to have her cut out of my will, and demanded a divorce from my wife. My wife was crying, my daughter was crying, a couple of other women (who apparently worked for her) were crying. I was angry. It was a mess.

I woke up from the dream exhausted.

But when I thought about it, all the scenes in my dream had some type of odd connection to something that had unfolded on that rather sordid Spanish historical TV series.

Needless to say, when it comes to my TV viewing, I'm moving on to something else.

> *Dreams are just thinking in a different*
> *biochemical state. In the sleep state, the brain*
> *thinks much more visually and intuitively.*
> — DEIRDRE BARRETT, HARVARD UNIVERSITY
> PSYCHOLOGIST, AUTHOR OF *THE COMMITTEE OF SLEEP*

I've always experienced remarkably vivid dreams. As an adolescent, I was a regular sleepwalker and was noted in my family for doing some very weird stuff while fast asleep. One night, I walked out of my bedroom, down a flight of stairs and into the dining room, pulled out a drawer from my mother's china cabinet, and urinated in the drawer.

Mom wasn't happy.

Another night found me walking down the stairs, out the front door, and into the street. Once in the street, I laid down right in the middle of the road and continued sleeping. By the grace of God, my father woke up after hearing the door slam behind me, ran outside, and found me, or I might not be here to write this book.

Although, thankfully, as I've grown, incidents have been much more rare, I've continued sleepwalking occasionally as an adult. A few years ago, I was traveling on business and checked into a hotel. After falling asleep, I woke up in the middle of the night to find myself standing in the middle of the hotel hallway—my hotel room door shut and locked behind me.

Fortunately, I don't sleep naked.

Those crazy moments don't happen much anymore, but they're a regular reminder of how little we understand about what's going on in our heads while we sleep.

I also have numerous recurring dreams, and sometimes even in the same night, I'll wake up, fall back asleep, and then pick up where the last dream left off. One recurring dream that's been going on for years and "drives" me crazy is finding myself driving a car backwards. For whatever reason, I'm careening down a hill, twisting my head, so I can see out the back, picking up speed, trying to avoid cars coming the other way, and I can't stop. I'll often wake up in a complete sweat from the stress of what it must feel like right before a massive car accident.

As a result of having so many vivid dreams, for years, I kept a dream journal, and every morning I would write down whatever I'd dreamed about the previous night—no matter how crazy and odd.

CAN DREAMS GIVE US CREATIVE INSIGHT?

For centuries, we've heard stories about amazing creative breakthroughs people have experienced during or after a dream. One of the most famous happened in 1869 when Russian chemist Dmitri Mendeleyev reported he dreamed about various elements coming together in a sequence. He woke up, jotted the elements down on a piece of paper, and out of that experience, the periodic table of elements was born, and we're still studying that table in high school.

In 1865, German chemist August Kekulé was struggling to understand the nature of the chemical benzene. In a strange dream where he reported seeing a snake swallowing its tail, he suddenly realized the image represented a visual diagram of the benzene molecule.

Many others have testified to the creative insights discovered in dreams from writers like Mary Shelley, author of *Frankenstein*, to inventors like Elias Howe, creator of the sewing machine. More recently, when he lay in bed in Rome during an illness working on his movie *Piranha II*, film director James Cameron dreamed of a horrifying robot walking out of a fire to attack a woman. Out of that experience, he wrote the screenplay and directed the film *Terminator*.

THE POWER OF A NAP

While many dreams happen in our deepest sleep phases, there is growing attention to dreams that happen right after falling asleep or right before waking up. These are often the kinds of dreams that happen when napping.

Artists like Salvador Dali, inventors like Thomas Edison, writers like Mary Shelley, and even physicist Albert Einstein understood the power of the stage of sleep we call "nodding off." At that moment, theta waves predominate in the brain, and over the years, many creative people have attributed that moment to a flush of breakthrough ideas.

These moments that some call being "half-asleep" can often reveal great insights. I've discovered that moments just before falling asleep as well as waking up have resulted in my most vivid dreams and occasionally reveal answers to problems I've been trying to overcome.

For me the key is to think about the problem right before falling asleep, but you have to be careful. If you start *ruminating* on the challenge, you won't be able to sleep at all. So I just remind myself of the problem I'm facing, so it's in my subconscious as I fall asleep.

Inventor Thomas Edison was a great proponent of napping. He was reported to only need four to five hours of sleep a night, but he discovered the power of those twilight moments going in and out of a nap. He actually experimented with sitting in a chair with a pair of steel ball bearings in his hands. He put metal plates under the chair so that when he dozed and dropped the ball bearings, the loud noise would wake him up. He was exploring what neuroscientists today call "hypnagogia" or "threshold consciousness"—that mysterious state between being awake and being asleep.

In a similar way, surrealist Salvador Dali scheduled thirty minutes each day for what he called "slumber with a key." In his version, he would hold a heavy key in his hand, and when it dropped on a plate, he would wake up like Edison. He claimed that it was those moments just before dropping the key that inspired his greatest work and described it in his book *50 Secrets of Magic Craftsmanship* as sufficient "for your whole physical and psychic being to be revivified by just the necessary amount of repose."

Today, there's plenty of research that backs up both Edison and Dali's ideas about the power of napping on creativity. So be aware of the sensations of falling asleep, and likewise, don't be so quick to leap out of bed in the morning or after a nap. Stay in the zone for a few minutes, and see what comes to the surface during those moments.

You may be surprised at the results.

> *A dream is a wish your heart makes,*
> *when you're fast asleep.*
> —WALT DISNEY, COFOUNDER OF WALT DISNEY STUDIOS

While amazing breakthroughs as the result of dreams have been reported, I think it's important to keep them in perspective. For all these remarkable examples, the truth is, dream researchers report that, considering the number of people out there and the number of dreams we experience, great creative breakthroughs are rare.

However, I believe the reason isn't because breakthroughs can't happen. It's because of two key reasons:

First, when it comes to creative breakthroughs while dreaming, our expectations are wrong. While I don't doubt those who report discovering complete answers to problems during a dream, from my experience, that's not how dreams work. More and more research indicates that dreams are about connecting things we would never think of connecting while we're conscious. As a result, we rarely get a clear answer while dreaming—it's more a revelation of something we never before considered. Understood in that way, we can learn to interpret those connections in a way that leads us to a breakthrough.

Second, most people haven't learned to remember their dreams. While I regularly wake up and share my weird dreams in excruciating detail, my wife only gets frustrated because she rarely remembers her dreams. Except for cases of those with neurological problems, it appears that everyone dreams—the problem is they have difficulty recalling their dreams upon waking. Remembering dreams is a choice and a technique that we'll discuss in a moment.

> *Dreaming is a unique form of sleep-dependent memory evolution, one that extracts new knowledge from existing information through the discovery and strengthening of unexpected and often previously unexplored associations.*
> —Antonio Zadra and Robert Stickgold,
> authors of *When Brains Dream*

I haven't kept a dream diary for many years, but I am scrupulous about keeping a notebook and pen on my nightstand. Since I discovered the unexpected *connections* my mind makes in the dream state, I'm *less* concerned about the bigger meaning of the dream narrative and *more* concerned about noting unusual associations, connections, or insights.

In other words, not every dream has a bigger meaning or lesson. While many psychologists believed Sigmund Freud's theories about dreams being based on *repressed longing* (the desires we're unable to express in polite company), most today don't believe every cylindrical object in a dream represents the penis or cave represents the vagina. Perhaps because Freud lived during the Victorian era, which was much more sexually repressed, he became obsessed with those ideas. However, in spite of all his theories, he admitted, "Sometimes, a cigar is just a cigar." Which means, stop obsessing about the bigger meaning of your dreams, and start looking more closely at the connections you hadn't thought of before the dream.

> **The question, "What does my dream mean?"
> may not be nearly as important as "What
> associations or connections happened in
> my dream that I haven't considered?"**

Now that we understand that, let's look more closely at how to remember our dreams. After all, no matter how many answers may lie in our dreams, it's all for naught if we can't remember them the next morning.

Dream researchers call this "dream incubation," and it's a technique I've used with great success. Admittedly, I still don't remember everything—particularly when I have multiple dreams—but following these ideas will help you do a much better job of remembering what's going on in your head while you're sleeping.

It's also worth noting that suffering an illness, being overly tired, or having drunk a little too much alcohol before bedtime doesn't help. Focus on nights where you're feeling good and have a clear head.

1) **Before you go to sleep, think about the specific problem you're trying to solve.** Don't go into great detail (once the brain starts working, it's hard to shut it down). But do consider the challenge and put it in your conscious mind. Think of your emotional response to the problem and the benefits of solving it. If it helps, jot it down in your notebook on the nightstand. Very often the act of writing it down makes a more indelible impression in your mind—which is also a good reminder to keep that pen and paper handy for writing down your insights later.

2) **Consciously tell yourself that you're going to remember the dream.** This isn't weird new-age advice, and you don't have to burn candles or incense. But it's important to remind yourself intentionally that your goal is to remember the dream. Trust me—it works.

3) **Go to sleep.**
4) **When you wake up, don't bounce out of bed or start thinking about your day.** Stay calm, keep your eyes closed, and do your best to remember your dreams. Give it a few minutes, and only when you have a good recollection of the dream, grab your notebook, and write it down. Even if you don't keep a specific dream journal, it will help your recall later to have a written record. You probably won't remember everything, but it's important to get down what you can.
5) **Don't get frustrated or discouraged.** You've probably spent years not being able to recall your dreams, so things won't change overnight. Keep at it. Practice matters. Plus, keep thinking about it during the day. I've experienced times when I couldn't remember a thing after waking up, but later in the day, pieces of the dream started popping into my head and things began coming together.

Be not afeard; the isle is full of noises, Sounds, and sweet airs, that give delight and hurt not. Sometimes a thousand twangling instruments Will hum about mine ears; and sometime voices, That, if I then had waked after long sleep, Will make me sleep again: and then, in dreaming, The clouds methought would open, and show riches Ready to drop upon me; that, when I waked, I cried to dream again.
—WILLIAM SHAKESPEARE, *THE TEMPEST*

Honestly, the vast majority of what I write down in my bedside notebooks are ideas that randomly pop into my head during the night. There's something about being fully relaxed and not dealing with the vast number of distractions of the day that opens our minds to new possibilities. In fact, it happens so often, I bought a pen with a tiny light on the tip, so I don't wake up my wife during my regular late-night note sessions.

So my advice is to start there.

And if your dreams begin to yield compelling connections, better yet. It's important to remember that you probably won't discover complete creative breakthroughs after awakening from a dream. More likely, you'll start seeing connections you weren't seeing before, and that's why writing them down and reflecting on your dreams is so important.

Most creative insights I've received from dreams only happened the next day or sometimes the next week as I thought more about the dream and reflected on the possibilities I remembered. Most of all, to engage your dreams to produce more creative revelations, think less about the mystical, romantic, or divine role they may play and more about the insights that might be revealed when you look seriously at unexpected associations and connections.

173

CHAPTER 23

BUILD IN THE TIME TO RECHARGE

"Remember the Sabbath day by keeping it holy. Six days you shall labor and do all your work, but the seventh day is a sabbath to the Lord your God. On it you shall not do any work, neither you, nor your son or daughter, nor your male or female servant, nor your animals, nor any foreigner residing in your towns. For in six days the Lord made the heavens and the earth, the sea, and all that is in them, but he rested on the seventh day.

"Therefore the Lord blessed the Sabbath day and made it holy."

—Exodus 20:8-11 (NIV)

I f you're old enough to remember working before the invention of the internet, you probably remember going home on Friday and rarely thinking about work over the weekend. Certainly there were exceptions during intense projects, but, for the most part, we weren't connected 24/7, weren't "always on," and by end of day Friday, we were unplugged until Monday morning.

The one thing I remember most about those days was how much energy and motivation I had walking into the office on Monday. I can even remember a growing anticipation that started on Sunday night as I looked toward the following week. Taking that time off had completely rejuvenated me, and my batteries were recharged and ready to go.

But today, not so much.

Because we've become virtual slaves to our electronic leashes, we now work straight through the weekends without giving it a second thought. If you're a professional creative, you probably already know the stats that reveal just how connected we are, but what bothers me the most is the chain reaction that happens every time we pick up our phone. Not only does it begin a screen session that can last for minutes at a time, but in 2019, a screen-tracking survey indicated that once we're done with that session, significant numbers of people pick up their phone *again* after only three minutes!

I saw one report recently on the number of people who actually touch their phone two thousand times a day. In fact, a recent study in the *Journal of the Association for Consumer Research* reported that even the presence of a turned-off smartphone lowered our cognitive performance. In other words, having our phone on the table—*even turned off*—during a meeting drops our level of thinking.

That chain reaction often begins with something *positive*— checking on my airline flight, worried about the weather, jotting down an idea, but then, before I realize it, I'm starting the end- less scroll through social media, and the zone out begins. Creative people know this better than anyone because procrastination is such a fearsome enemy. It's just *so much* easier to check our email, text messages, social media, and other trivial pursuits while we put off the hard work of what really matters. And that doesn't count office interruptions, phone calls, meetings, and the waterfall of other distractions throughout our day.

THE POWER OF A WEEKLY BREAK

Today, we carry around an office connection in our pocket, so we're never really unplugged from work, email, or social media. Sitting in the doctor's waiting room or waiting in line at a store, I don't let my mind wander, daydream, or observe the people around me—it's too easy to pull out my phone and start scrolling. We do it without thinking and do it in the evenings, on the weekends, and even on vacation.

This is why we've completely lost that energy and sense of anticipation on Monday morning. Now, our workday goes seven days a week; there's no letup and no retreat.

Athletes know that if they train 24/7 without a rest, their body will break down. The same thing is happening to most of our minds. Human beings weren't created to be "always on," and without some kind of rest, our brain and our spirit will break down as well.

That's why I'm such a strong believer in the power of the Sabbath.

> *We don't know where we get our ideas from. What we do know is that we do not get them from our laptops.*
> —JOHN CLEESE, ACTOR AND COMEDIAN

The concept of a "Sabbath" or *Shabbat* in Hebrew was an important part of the creation story in the Bible's book of Genesis, where the seventh day is set aside as a day of rest and made holy by God (Genesis 2:2–3). It was important enough to be included again by Moses in the Ten Commandments. On the seventh day, God rested from creating the world, and taught that practice in the biblical commandment of Exodus 20:8 (NIV): "Remember the sabbath day, to keep it holy." That command expanded from the Jewish and Christian world to other religions as well as secular communities. The weekend eventually became a legally protected time for rest, recreation, and religious practice, and in some countries, that includes Friday night as well. The five-day workweek was instituted by labor unions originally attempting to accommodate Jewish workers in New England cotton mills, and it was also embraced by Henry Ford in 1926.

It grew to become a standard practice in America around 1940. and China came late to the table when they adopted it in 2006. Today, most of the world has adopted an internationally sanctioned work schedule—either by law or common acceptance—recognizing the need to take off at least one day a week for rest.

> *The real issue is not the number of hours we sit*
> *behind a desk but the energy we bring to the work*
> *we do and the value we generate as a result.*
> —TONY SCHWARTZ, *HOW TO BE EXCELLENT AT ANYTHING*

In 2005, *National Geographic* traveled around the world to learn the secrets of living a long and productive life. One of the most interesting subjects were Seventh-day Adventists in Loma Linda, California. Among other things, Seventh-day Adventists take the practice of a Sabbath seriously, and the research points to that as a major reason for their longevity. In fact, not only are they more healthy, but they tend to live four to ten years longer than others in California.

Another study in 2014 by the School of Public Health at Loma Linda University pointed to the connection between Sabbath-keeping and mental health. Their work indicated that "refraining from secular activities on Sabbath was associated with better mental health and better physical health."

If you only think the idea of a Sabbath is for religious people, then think again.

Writing for the Religious News Service, Emily McFarlan Miller profiled the story of Tiffany Shlain, founder of the Webby Awards. Since the Webby Awards celebrate *online* excellence, Tiffany literally built her career by being online, along with running a film studio. But she came to the point that something had to be done.

Miller reported:

> *Every Friday evening for nearly a decade, Shlain and her family have unplugged their devices and spent the next 24 hours offline in what she calls a "Technology Shabbat." "As our society becomes more oversaturated with technology, I feel like it's the thing we need right now," she said.*

Miller goes on to write:

> *Tech Shabbat is a modern twist on an ancient religious practice, which is attracting the attention of burned-out millennials and others who are exhausted by trying to keep up in an increasingly connected and fast-paced world. And there's some science to support the idea that practicing a day of rest—including time away from social media and digital devices—benefits longevity and both mental and physical health. It's a practice that can benefit people of faith and those who don't believe, alike. "This can be adapted for anyone, wherever you fall on the belief spectrum, and it will bring meaning and value to your life in unbelievable ways," Shlain said.*

> **One day a week I seek to rest from earthly toil and sorrow.**
> **Revitalized, I find the strength to battle new tomorrows.**
> —RICHELLE E. GOODRICH, *SLAYING*
> *DRAGONS: QUOTES, POETRY, & A FEW SHORT*
> *STORIES FOR EVERY DAY OF THE YEAR*

Certainly there are times during the day—even when the clock is ticking and the pressure is on—when the best option is to unplug and take a break. With the Sabbath, we're talking about making it a weekly ritual. While the rules of keeping an orthodox Jewish version of the Sabbath can be quite extensive, I'm talking about starting with a *technology* Sabbath.

Just unplug for one day a week, and see what happens.

Go out to eat, enjoy friends (in person), watch a ballgame, go to the lake, attend church, shop—but forget about work. Forget about the pressure of the big idea you have to deliver, and forget about answering the long list of emails in your inbox. Just unwind and enjoy.

But what will my boss, my friends, my clients, and my associates think?

If you've been a hardcore, 24/7, workaholic, I'm not going to lie. It won't be easy—especially at first. But remember, all of those bosses, clients, friends, and others became so demanding because you trained them to be demanding. Because you answered emails and text messages immediately, they've grown to assume that will always happen. Because you answer your phone every time it rings, they assume you'll pick it up every time they call.

You trained them to turn you into a workaholic, and you'll need to train them to change their perceptions of you and the way you work.

Start today. Stop responding immediately or after normal working hours. You may get the shakes at first, but you'll eventually get used to it. Give that email, text message, or phone message a little time before you return it.

Eventually they'll get the idea. They'll learn to understand your schedule (and your priorities) have changed. And remember, be gracious during the process. You don't have to explain to everyone or become annoyed. People will need time to adjust, so be intentional, but stick to your schedule.

*When practiced, Sabbath-keeping is an active protest
against a culture that is always on, always available
and always looking for something else to do.*
—STEPHEN W. SMITH, *INSIDE JOB: DOING
THE WORK WITHIN THE WORK*

You may actually enjoy being on 24/7, but I can guarantee you, it's hurting your creativity. Particularly when it comes to developing breakthrough ideas on demand, without the occasional recharge of the batteries, we'll all run out of power.

Cal Newport, author of *Deep Work: Rules for Focused Success in a Distracted World,* says it well:

> *Decades of work from multiple different subfields within psychology all point toward the conclusion that regularly resting your brain improves the quality of your deep work. When you work, work hard. When you're done, be done. Your average e-mail response time might suffer some, but you'll more than make up for this with the sheer volume of truly important work produced during the day by your refreshed ability to dive deeper than your exhausted peers.[12]*

---

12 Cal Newport, *Deep Work: Rules for Focused Success in a Distracted World* (New York: Grand Central Publishing, 2016).

CHAPTER 24

HOW TO MAKE YOUR DREAM THEIR DREAM

HOW TO SUCCESSFULLY PITCH YOUR IDEAS

When we are selling our ideas, the audience must first buy us.

—Peter Coughter, *The Art of the Pitch: Persuasion and Presentation Skills that Win Business*

O ne of the big reasons we struggle with creating ideas on a dead-line is our inability to present those ideas to the boss, the client, or the team. No matter how great your idea or how quickly you come up with it, if you can't express it well, it hardly matters, and certainly, no one is going to get excited about it.

In fact, the best idea in the world is worthless if you can't get the people who can make it happen passionate about it. Even for the creative lone wolves out there, you'll eventually need an investor or donor, publisher, distributor, manufacturer, and potentially more to actually bring that idea to reality.

In many ways, the ability to present or "pitch" your ideas is one of the most important things you can learn in business—or life. Whether you're trying to produce a movie, publish a book, get a raise, launch a business, find donors, or whatever, your ability to inspire others to your way of thinking is critical to your success.

PITCHING TO *RELATIONSHIPS* PEOPLE VERSUS *RESULTS* PEOPLE

One of the keys to successful pitching is understanding the person on the other end of the pitch. When it comes to presentations, there are usually two kinds of people: *relationship* people and *results* people. Relationship people like to talk. They like the interchange. It takes a while to get around to your project because they want to chat about the weather, your kids, the big game last night—anything. Meetings with relationship people can be 90 percent chitchat and 10 percent substance, and they usually last longer. Think of buying something from a street vendor in the Middle East. It's a complete opera—waving hands, arguing back and forth, lots of activity—all just to buy an apple.

That's a relationship person.

On the other hand, I'm a results person.

My mantra is "Don't tell me how deep the water is; just bring in the boat." I want you to get to the point, and don't bore me with the details. You may have lovely children, but results people don't need to hear about them. They just want to know why you're taking up their time.

While results people can be jerks, most of them are incredibly nice—they're just more concerned about the project than everything else.

It's not really a matter of one style being better or worse; it's a matter of recognizing the difference in the way people are wired. And knowing that information can mean the difference between success and failure when it comes to pitching your ideas.

WHAT SHOULD I DO IF THERE'S AN UNEXPECTED GUEST?

If you're a creative professional, then you know pitching projects or ideas is difficult—even in the best situation. Whether it's a movie idea, a design project, real estate, a new job—whatever, there are so many variables that, even with experience, it's always a challenge. One of the most common challenges in pitching is *the presence of an expected guest*.

Here's the scenario: For weeks, you've been preparing to pitch to "Mr. Big." You've done your homework, you know the details, and you are ready to go. But when you arrive, you're surprised by the presence of *another* person in the room with Mr. Big. Sometimes he or she is introduced, and sometimes not—so you don't know if it's another producer, a partner in the firm, a romantic relationship, a golfing buddy, or your competition.

Whoever it is, it's terribly awkward.

So most creative people decide the best strategy is to focus on Mr. Big. After all, he invited you, and he (or she) is the one who can approve the project. So it makes perfect sense.

Wrong.

The problem is, no matter who that mystery guest is, the first thing Mr. Big will do when you walk out of the room is turn to that person and ask, "So, what did you think?" And if you ignored or disrespected that guest, she'll probably respond with, "Honestly, I didn't like her very much."

And your project is dead.

Here's the key: Whenever you pitch and there's an unexpected guest present, introduce yourself, and then pitch to both people. Embrace the guest(s) and include them in your presentation. You have no idea the influence they may have with Mr. Big, so impressing *them* can be just as important as impressing *him*.

DON'T LET REJECTION GET THE BEST OF YOU

Someone pitched me a project the other day. He had obviously worked very hard on it and was very passionate. But he made one serious mistake: He let his passion spill over into annoyance and then arrogance. After giving me a long speech about his credentials and why his experience justified my listening to his pitch, he then went into a diatribe about what was wrong with people in Hollywood and why they haven't responded to him. I understood his frustration because, after all, I've been out here for decades working in the industry and been rejected plenty of times, so I get it.

But honestly, he got rather demanding about me reading his proposal. So I mentioned that I have a stack of proposals, scripts, and projects that come into our office on a regular basis, and I'd read it over at the next available opportunity.

While I appreciated his passion, he was absolutely convinced his project was the next big thing, so the conversation went downhill from there. He said, "All the other scripts you receive are from amateurs, and mine isn't, so you should read this."

I could go on and on, but the bottom line was he wanted me to set aside our own projects, other people's proposals, and take the time out of my schedule to read through his project, respond, and eventually produce it. I don't have a big development team, so I told him I'd have to put it in line. He stormed out of the office, and that was the last communication I had with him (which was fine with me).

The lesson? I'm sure this guy was a good guy and meant well. But when you pitch a movie, book, or other project—even when you've been rejected multiple times—don't become pushy, angry, or bitter. It simply doesn't help your cause to get frustrated at the person you're trying to win over. I know it's tough out there because we pitch our own projects at Cooke Media Group on a regular basis. But trust me—arrogance doesn't help gain support.

Whenever I encounter someone like this, I always remember the late Ken Wales, producer of films like *Amazing Grace, Revenge of the Pink Panther,* and *Captive.* Many years ago, he was pitching the idea of taking Catherine Marshall's best-selling novel *Christy* and turning it into a movie. He pitched and pitched and got rejection after rejection. Years went by, and his *Christy* movie idea was all Ken would talk about. I can't imagine the frustration he felt after so many closed (and sometimes slammed) doors.

I even pulled him aside at one point as a friend and said, "Ken, give it a rest. Nobody wants to produce a movie about a turn-of-the-century farm girl." But Ken wouldn't give up. He stayed positive and cheerful, and I never once saw him angry, resentful, or bitter.

Then, after years and years of pitching, Jeff Sagansky, then president of CBS Television, bought it as a TV series, and it ran successfully for years.

No matter how frustrated you become, just remember Ken. Never become a jerk, and never, ever let them see you sweat.

HOW TO MAKE A GREAT PITCH

So, how can you make *your* dream *their* dream? How can you get them as excited as you are about your idea? To make you better at presenting your brilliant projects, here are nine important principles to keep in mind:

1) **Someone once said, "A good idea is the worst thing in the world if it's the only one you've got."** If possible, always bring in three to five ideas to present. In my experience, they rarely buy into the first idea out of the gate, but if one idea is all you have, the

meeting is over. I've often been successful with idea two or three, so no matter how excited you are about idea number one, always be ready to present a number of potential concepts.

2) **Do your homework.** Learn everything you can about the person on the other side of the table. Check industry magazines, trade journals, websites, referrals, etc. Get as much information about him or her as you can before you walk into the room, and whatever you do, never go in blind. I once knew a producer who forgot this principle and pitched a horror movie to a production company that only produced family movies. Bad idea.

3) **Even though it might take some time, if possible, don't just pitch—try to develop a personal friendship.** When that happens, it's less awkward, and you have more access. Early in my career I had the opportunity to pitch some scripts to a very successful producer. One by one, she turned them all down, but it turned out we had a number of mutual friends, and over the next few months, that awkward meeting eventually developed into a friendship. Now, I don't need to go through the uncomfortable process of scheduling a meeting and doing a formal pitch. I just call her up and ask her advice about my idea.

4) **Speaking of asking for advice, instead of just trying to sell them, start by genuinely asking for their opinions and advice.** Going in with that goal takes the pressure off them, and you'll be surprised how much it helps. That producer, publisher, investor, or whoever is on the other side of the table feels as awkward during a pitch as you. So rather than forcing him or her to say yes or no, you can make it far more comfortable by going in with the purpose of simply asking their opinion of your idea. And for the record, you'd be amazed at how many times I've asked for advice or opinions about projects, and once they heard about it, they wanted to get involved!

5) **These are busy people, so do your best to limit the presentation, and please don't show up late.** Honor the appointment time. I actually have a friend who asks for fifteen minutes to pitch an idea, and at the end of the fifteen minutes, even if the meeting is going well, he excuses himself and leaves! It sounds rude, but the funny thing is he gets asked back again and again because executives know how much he respects their time.

6) **A script, treatment, photos, or demonstrations can potentially help, but don't get cute.** The slickest presentation rarely wins. Over the years, I've had someone make me listen to his piano version of the movie soundtrack, and once, an eager filmmaker showed me watercolor paintings he'd done of every major scene in his film! Remember that the higher level the person you're pitching to, the more they're concerned with content, not packaging. And if you do bring a handout such as a script, treatment, sketch, or written proposal, don't give it out until the end. Otherwise, they'll be reading it and not listening to you.

7) **After the meeting, give them time to think about it.** Don't follow up too soon, or it will drive them crazy. I once heard a pitch for a TV program, and the producer literally called me on his way home from his car to ask if I'd made a decision. Give them a week or two at least. Call or email them every day, and you'll burn that bridge.

8) **Learn to listen.** I once successfully pitched a documentary film to a producer without saying a word. I walked into the producer's office while he was literally screaming at someone else on the phone. I stood there quietly, and as I listened, I realized that on the other end of the call was the director of his last project who went over budget and way beyond the schedule. The producer was absolutely furious. After about ten minutes of ranting, he slammed down the phone and pulled himself together. A little embarrassed, he looked up at me, explained the situation, and

said, "Thanks for being so patient. Tell you what. I'll do whatever it is you want to produce." I walked away with the project without saying much more than thank you. So remember, a successful pitch isn't just about you dominating the conversation.

9) **Before you walk in the door, know what "success" means to them.** We often get so focused on what we want out of the meeting that we forget to think about what will motivate them to be involved. For instance, sometimes in Hollywood, movie studios aren't as interested in making a profit as much as winning an Academy Award. So if your project can help them achieve that goal, then they're ready. A business executive might be more interested in fame than money. A donor might want his or her name on a building. Understand their motivation and plan your presentation around that.

Perhaps more than anything, know that successful presenting isn't an act. The people hearing your presentation are smart and experienced and can smell a "con" a mile away. Be real, and be you.

It will make a big difference.

PART 4

THE MOMENTUM
THE ART OF UNLEASHING CREATIVITY IN OTHERS

What kind of paragons are the men and women who run successful [advertising] agencies? My observation has been that they are enthusiasts. They are intellectually honest. They have the guts to face tough decisions. They are resilient in adversity. Most of them are natural charmers. They are not bullies. They encourage communications upwards, and are good listeners.

—David Ogilvy, advertising executive

CHAPTER 25

ATMOSPHERE MATTERS: HOW TO DESIGN A CREATIVE CULTURE

Starbucks was founded around the experience and the environment of their stores. Starbucks was about a space with comfortable chairs, lots of power outlets, tables and desks at which we could work and the option to spend as much time in their stores as we wanted without any pressure to buy. The coffee was incidental.
— Simon Sinek, author, motivational speaker, and marketing consultant

N ow that you've learned some of the most effective ways to unleash your creative potential when it's needed the most, it's important to understand the atmosphere it takes to keep the idea factory working. This last section is focused on principles that will help you nurture those ideas, get others excited about them, and build confidence in the future.

You may be working on your own right now, but as you move forward in your creative career, you'll discover more and more opportunities to be a leader of *other* creative professionals. Thanks to great leadership teachers like John Maxwell, Patrick Lencioni, Jack Welch, Seth Godin, and others, there are fantastic books and other resources out there on leadership. However, when it comes to leading *creative* people, the story is a little different.

While that subject would make another book, I wanted to include this bonus section to at least get you started on the journey. Hopefully, this section will help prepare you for that moment, and it's important to begin with how to build a creative culture for your team and your organization.

It's no secret that culture is more important than vision.

I've worked in creative, vibrant organizational cultures where original thinking was valued and wonderful things happened. On the other hand, I've worked at organizations where you could literally feel the oppression when you walked into the building. Those destructive cultures often have leaders with great vision and potential, but because the culture is so negative, that vision will never be realized.

Since those days, I've focused a significant part of my career on discovering the secrets to building creative, vibrant cultures. In that process, I've learned ten critical principles to turn around numerous organizations. Many ideas on this list I've shared earlier, but it's important to rethink them in terms of building a creative culture:

1) **Create stability**—Creative people need stability. If they're worried about losing their job, financial problems, or excessive turnover, they'll never release their best ideas. I've seen terrible leaders think they're motivating the team by threatening them with being fired or telling them they'll be blamed if the company goes out of business—which is the worst thing you could ever do.

   Even when you're going through difficult times, create an atmosphere of stability for the team. That doesn't mean you lie, but you search for the positive inside the negative. No matter how dire the situation, leaders need to surround the creative team with a positive purpose.

   You'll be rewarded down the road.

2) **Make it safe from excessive criticism**—Critics are a dime a dozen, but leaders who can help their team move from bad ideas to legendary ideas are rare. There's a time to look at what doesn't work, but that should be done in an atmosphere of trust. Criticism always goes down better when it comes from a trusted and respected source.

   That sometimes means separating the creative team from other departments. Many times, employees in other departments don't quite get how the creative process works. As a result, they can become jealous about their crazy offices, different working hours, or relaxed attitudes. In those cases, they often criticize because they don't understand. Once again, the leader needs to protect the creative team from inside and outside criticism.

3) **Make sure your leaders are on the same page**—All it takes is one of your leaders to contradict what you're trying to do to wreck a creative culture. At the beginning of building your culture, make absolutely sure your leadership team is unified and moving with you. One critical or disconnected leader or manager can sow seeds of doubt that will topple the entire project.

I've been hired by leaders and spent time with them going over their vision and goals for the project. But the next day, I got a call from another high-level leader in the same organization who said, "Now, what the CEO asked you to do yesterday isn't exactly what we need." Then he proceeded to cast a completely different vision

That leads to catastrophe. Creative people need to pursue a unified vision, so make sure before you engage creative people, every leader in the business, nonprofit, church, or other organization is on the same page.

4) **Be flexible**—Creative people don't all operate on the same schedule or work the same way. Give your team some flexibility, and it will revolutionize their attitude. At one major nonprofit, I talked the CEO into allowing the creative team to rip up carpet, repaint, dump the cubicles, and design their own work spaces. There was fear and trembling on the CEO's part, but within a matter of months, the creative team transformed the organization.

A very traditional small market TV station brought in a hot young designer who dressed, acted, and looked different than anyone else in the organization. He essentially freaked everyone out, and a very vocal group of older employees demanded he be fired. But I knew his potential and talked the station manager into letting him work from home—far away from the old school thinkers and critics.

Within six months, his designs had completely turned around that TV station. Creative people come in all sizes, shapes, attitudes, skill levels and more, so let them stretch your thinking.

5) **Get them the tools they need**—Nothing drags a creative team down as much as broken, old, or out-of-date tools. Sure, we all have budget challenges, but do whatever you can to get them the right computers, design tools, video equipment—and whatever else they need.

Granted, part of the excitement and allure of a startup is launching with limited resources. But once that initial excitement is over, that enthusiasm wanes quickly when we're dealing with old or inadequate equipment, office supplies, or other resources.

I've said it before: the less time and energy they spend overcoming technical and equipment problems, the more time and energy they can spend on developing amazing ideas.

6) **Push them outside their comfort zone**—Leaders often think that creative people want to be left alone and operate on their own schedule. Sure, they like to create their own timetable, but they also relish a challenge. In fact, while they probably won't admit it, remember my principle that most creative people actually love deadlines because it gives them perspective on the project. I don't even like to start working until I can see the deadline approaching. There is just something about a challenge that gets my blood flowing and the ideas coming.

A little fear in the face of a great challenge can inspire creative teams.

7) **Get out of their way**—One of the most important aspects of a creative culture, once it's in process, is to get out of the way of your creative team. We all know micromanaging is a disaster for anyone—especially creatives—so give them space and let them solve problems on their own.

This is particularly difficult when it comes to leaders of creative people. Face it—successful results from the creative team are generally more exciting than successful results from the accounting team. So it's natural for leaders to want to be seen as part of that work. But the truth is, leaders will get credit because they're leaders, so fight the fear that you'll be left out of getting proper credit.

Set the stage well, and then get out of the way, and let them fly. That's the best way to win respect.

8) **Understand the difference between organizational structure and communication structure**—This is a huge issue for me. Every organization needs an organizational structure. Who reports to whom matters, and hierarchy is important. Without a proper organizational chart most organizations would end up in chaos. Even with a "flat" management model, understanding the order and flow of any company or nonprofit matters.

When it comes to communication, I recommend you throw the organizational structure out the window. Your creative team should be able to call anyone to ask questions and discuss ideas. Don't force them to communicate through supervisors, managers, or anyone else.

In one organization, the designer of a new logo was forced to wait for months as approvals traveled through nine layers of managers, department heads, and vice presidents until the logo could get to the CEO for the final sign-off. The process took thirty-seven revisions over nine months. Needless to say, it was a disaster.

Create a free-flowing communication system, and the ideas will grow.

9) **Walk the factory floor**—Leadership expert John Maxwell recommends that leaders "walk the factory floor" and meet every employee. Develop a personal relationship with employees at all levels—especially when it comes to your creative team. Former Pixar and Disney Animation president Ed Catmull took that seriously—even when it came to giving bonuses. When they produced a box-office success, they'd share the profits with the team that produced it—which often included a great number of people. But Ed didn't just mail or directly deposit the check and send a nice note. Ed took the time to either go to each team member personally or invite them to his office individually to hand them the check—and tell them how much their work was appreciated.

10) **Give them credit**—Finally, a great creative culture allows everyone to be noticed for their accomplishments. Never take credit for your team's work, and always give them the honor they're due. You'll find that when you protect your creative team and allow them to get the glory for their work, they'll follow you into a fire.

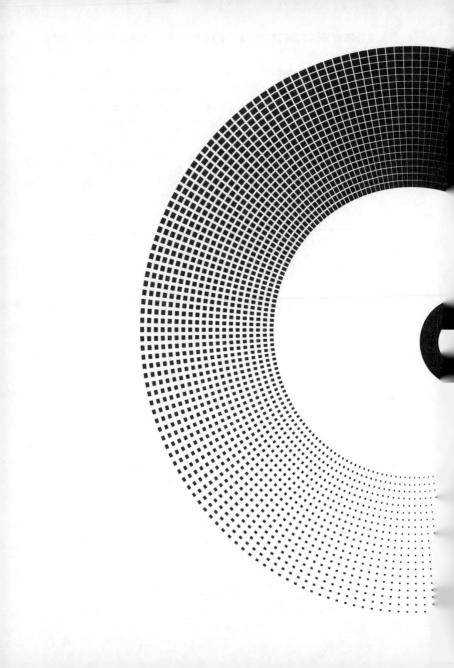

CHAPTER 26

LEADING HIGH ACHIEVERS

*My job is not to be easy on people. My job
is to take these great people we have and to
push them and make them even better.*

—STEVE JOBS, FOUNDER OF APPLE COMPUTER

As a creative leader, at some point in your career, you'll have
the influence, budget, and resources to build a team of high
achievers. High achievers come in all packages and personality
types and can revolutionize organizations. However, what I find more
often is that bosses discover pretty quickly they are way out of their
depth when it comes to managing that kind of brilliant, high-energy
team—or worse, they become intimidated by their talent. Either way,
it's a crisis waiting to happen.

As a creative leader, at some point in your career you'll have the influence, budget, and resources to build a team of high achievers.

When you get to that point in your career—or if you're already there—here's a handful of good tips for maximizing your leadership ability with high-achieving teams:

1) **Start with yourself.** High achievers respect leaders who have high standards, perform well under pressure, and can inspire teams even in the most difficult circumstances. You'll never lead high achievers well if you can't lead yourself.

2) **Treat them differently from low achievers.** Far too often, we want to treat everyone the same, but with high achievers, that's a recipe for disaster. Moral principles teach that we respect everyone equally because we are all unique human beings in the sight of God. However, that doesn't mean our gifts, talents, and skills are equal. When it comes to salaries, office hours, rules, freedom, perks, and other job-related issues, each person on the team should be rewarded based on their value to the project.

3) **Give them the resources they need, and then get out of the way.** I mentioned this earlier, and it's worth mentioning again. You're only shooting yourself in the foot when you don't give high achievers the resources they need. Micromanaging is the worst thing you can do with these high performers. So don't let your insecurities as a leader get in the way of allowing them to fly.

4) **Separate them from low achievers.** In most cases, nothing will drive a high achiever crazy faster than having to work next to a low achiever. My advice? Put them on a different floor, in a different room, or better yet—in a different building than the other members of your team.

I will admit that, occasionally, it's a smart thing to couple high achievers with low achievers—particularly if they're friends, have worked together before, and complement each other's skill set. For instance, a high-level creative partnering with a lower-level organizer could be a plus. However, skill sets and attitudes are two different things. If a low achiever's attitude or lazy performance is driving a high achiever crazy, they'll need some serious space between them.

5) **Pay them what they're worth, and stop nitpicking your best people.** Sure, we want to think creative people are working for you because of loyalty or the "cause," but people have to pay their bills. Obviously, budgets are a challenge for everyone, but when you do have the resources, by holding back financially with your best people, you're killing a big part of their motivation. If your budget is limited, perhaps more time off, working from home, or other perks will help. Whatever works for you, just remember that with creative people, rewards matter.

None of these ideas needs to be overdone or cause tension in your organization. But through skillful leadership, you can take your high achievers to even higher levels and, in the process, transform your organization.

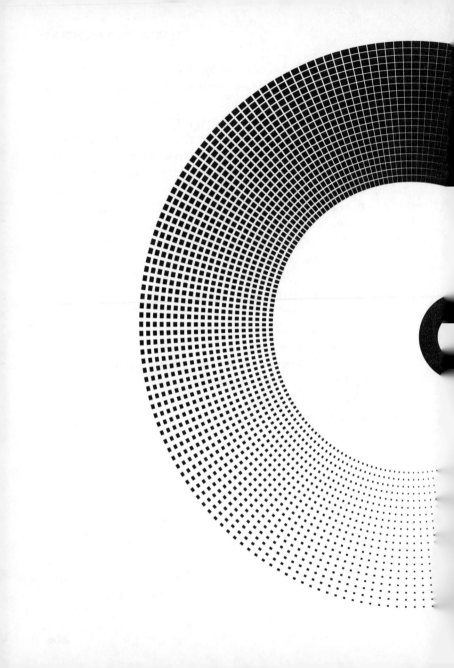

CHAPTER 27

YOUR IDEAS SHOULD GET PEOPLE TALKING

Creativity is contagious. Pass it on.

—Albert Einstein, physicist

t was in high school that I started making movies. It was a pathetic affair, really. I had my dad's Super-8 movie camera and a group of friends who were crazy enough to try anything, so that's all it took.

We started out by fooling around with the camera, learning how it worked, and our first film was just a mash-up of smashing each other with raw eggs, making silly faces, and fake fighting. But we learned how to shoot, and it didn't take long before we were hooked.

During our high school years, we produced mafia movies, war movies, space movies—and since we didn't know how to actually edit film, staging action scenes (especially fights) was quite elaborate. We loved it, but it never crossed our minds that filmmaking was something you could do for a living.

After high school, I went a thousand miles away to college and thought I might find some new friends to make movies with, so I packed up my little three-minute movies (that's all a reel could hold back then), my Super-8 camera, and took off. I enrolled as a music major because I played the piano (after all, my dad was a pastor, and when you're a preacher's kid, playing piano is part of the job description.)

Plus, I had no other ideas for what in the world I wanted to do with my life.

Literally, the first day at the university, I was unpacking my suitcases in the dorm, and a couple of my film reels fell out on the floor. A guy across the hall named Rod Carlson noticed, introduced himself, and told me he was taking a film class, and if I were interested, he'd take me down to the university film department and show me how to actually edit my movies.

So that night, we sat in the media department in front of a film editing console and started work. I was having the time of my life, and I was so engrossed in learning how to edit, I didn't realize the film professor was also there working on a project of his own.

Late in the evening, the professor was leaving, but he stopped at our editing booth, introduced himself, and said he had been watching my film over our shoulders, and to my shock, was impressed.

He told us he had students who had been taking film classes for years and still weren't doing the kind of work I had shown in my little film. So he asked if he could show my movie in his class the next day.

I replied that would be great—if I could sit on the back row of the class.

The next day I showed up in class, the professor threaded my film through the projector, and the students sat back and watched. Trust me—this wasn't Academy Award material, and I wasn't sure what their reaction would be.

But at the end of the film, in spite of it being amateurish, they started talking about it. These people I had never met were discussing my movie! I'd never had an experience like that before, and it was at that exact moment that I had a crystal-clear revelation like I've never had before or since.

The thought hit me that if I could do something creative with a camera that made people talk like this, then that's exactly what I was supposed to do with my life.

When I left that class, I went straight to the registrar's office and changed my major, so I could study film and media, and I've never looked back.

My challenge to you is to create ideas that will get people talking. In today's disconnected, distracted, and polarized world, just getting people engaging with each other is a great start.

And that's exactly what great ideas do.

You've been given the gift of creativity, and now you have the tools to create breakthrough ideas in the real world of deadlines and pressure.

Now, go and use it, and in the process, *get people talking.*

Because that's the way to change the world.

CHAPTER 28

GOING DEEPER

*In the case of good books, the point is not to see
how many of them you can get through, but
rather how many can get through to you.*

—Mortimer J. Adler, founder, The Great
Books of the Western World Program

This book was written for working professionals who need practical answers under the gun. As a result, I made it short and sweet. However, I would also encourage you to go deeper.

I also must make a confession that I'm far more creative when I'm spending time reading. Studying the lives of brilliant men and women and the development of their ideas inspires and motivates me more than anything else. I've been pursuing a creative career for a long time and have seen numerous books and other resources over the years. While there are a few of those classics on this list, the majority reflect the most recent research on the subjects we've discussed in these pages. While there are many more I'd love to add, this is a good place to start, and I'd encourage you to continue your creative journey by checking them out.

RECOMMENDED READING

Alter, Adam. *Irresistible: The Rise of Addictive Technology and the Business of Keeping US Hooked*. Penguin Books, 2018.

Berger, Warren. *A More Beautiful Question: The Power of Inquiry to Spark Breakthrough Ideas*. Langara College, 2019.

Block, Peter. *The Answer to How Is Yes: Acting on What Matters*. Berrett-Koehler, 2003.

Bond, Michael. *From Here to There: The Art and Science of Finding and Losing Our Way*. Belknap Harvard, 2021.

Burkus, David. *The Myths of Creativity: The Truth about How Innovative Companies and People Generate Great Ideas*. Jossey-Bass, 2014.

Catmull, Edwin E., and Amy Wallace. *Creativity, Inc.: Overcoming the Unseen Forces That Stand in the Way of True Inspiration*. Random House, 2014.

Cloud, Henry. *Changes That Heal: The Four Shifts That Make Everything Better . . . and That Anyone Can Do*. Zondervan, 1992.

The Copy Book: How Some of the Best Advertising Writers in the World Write Their Advertising. Taschen, 2021.

Cox, Christopher. *The Deadline Effect: How to Work like It's the Last Minute - Before the Last Minute*. Avid Reader Pr, 2022.

Currey, Mason. *Daily Rituals: How Artists Work*. Alfred A. Knopf, 2016.

Dickens, Charles. *Night Walks: And Other Essays*. Read & Co., 2020.

Duggan, William R., and Amy Murphy. *The Art of Ideas: Creative Thinking for Work and Life*. Columbia University Press, 2020.

Eurich, Tasha. *Insight: Why We're Not as Self-Aware as We Think, and How Seeing Ourselves Clearly Helps Us Succeed at Work and in Life.* Crown Business, 2017.

Galenson, David W. *Old Masters and Young Geniuses: The Two Life Cycles of Artistic Creativity.* Princeton University Press, 2006.

Gardner, John Champlin. *The Art of Fiction: Notes on Craft for Young Writers.* Vintage, 1991.

Godin, Seth. *The Practice: Shipping Creative Work.* Portfolio, 2020.

Grant, Alec. *Originals: How Non-Conformists Change the World.* Penguin, 2016.

Hahn, Don. *Brain Storm: Unleashing Your Creative Self.* Disney Editions, 2011.

Harfoush, Rahaf. *Hustle & Float: Reclaim Your Creativity and Thrive in a World Obsessed with Work.* Diversion Books, 2019.

Henry, Todd. *The Accidental Creative: How to Be Brilliant at a Moment's Notice.* Gildan Audio Imprint, 2014.

Huth, John Edward. *The Lost Art of Finding Our Way.* The Belknap Press of Harvard University Press, 2015.

Judkins, Rod. *The Art of Creative Thinking: 89 Ways to See Things Differently.* Perigee Books, 2016.

Kelley, Tom, and David Kelley. *Creative Confidence: Unleashing the Creative Potential within Us All.* William Collins, 2015.

Kierkegaard, Søren, and Charles E. Moore. *Provocations: Spiritual Writings.* Plough Publishing House, 2014.

Kounios, John, and John Beeman. *Eureka Factor: Creative Insights and the Brain: Aha Moments, Creative Insight, and the Brain.* Windmill Books, 2016.

Mack, Karin. *Overcoming Writing Blocks.* Penguin Books, 1980.

MacLeod, Hugh. *Ignore Everybody: And 39 Other Keys to Creativity*. Penguin, 2010.

Monahan, Tom. *The Do-It-Yourself Lobotomy: Open Your Mind to Greater Creative Thinking*. John Wiley & Sons, 2002.

Newport, Cal. *Deep Work: Rules for Focused Success in a Distracted World*. Grand Central Publishing, 2016.

Ogilvy, David. *Ogilvy on Advertising*. Prion, 2011.

Ogilvy, David. *Unpublished David Ogilvy*. Profile Books Ltd, 2012.

Paul, Annie Murphy. *The Extended Mind: The Power of Thinking Outside the Brain*. Houghton Mifflin Harcourt, 2021.

Pressfield, Steven. *The War of Art*. Orion, 2003.

Prochnik, George. *In Pursuit of Silence: Listening for Meaning in a World of Noise*. Anchor Books, 2011.

Solnit, Rebecca. *A Field Guide to Getting Lost*. Langara College, 2018.

Solnit, Rebecca. *Wanderlust: A History of Walking*. Granta Books, 2021.

Sullivan, Luke, and Edward Boches. *Hey Whipple, Squeeze This: The Classic Guide to Creating GREAT ADS: Includes Digital, Social, and Emerging Media*. Wiley, 2016.

West, Thomas G. *Seeing What Others Cannot See: The Hidden Advantages of Visual Thinkers and Differently Wired Brains*. Prometheus Books, 2017.

Young, James Webb. *A Technique for Producing Ideas*. McGraw-Hill, 2007.

Zadra, Antonio. *When Brains Dream: Exploring the Science and Mystery of Sleep*. W. W. Norton, 2022.

FIND OUT MORE ABOUT PHIL COOKE:

To learn more about Phil Cooke, start with his blog at:

PHILCOOKE.COM

Or his company website at Cooke Media Group:

COOKEMEDIAGROUP.COM

The *Phil Cooke Podcast* is available on iTunes, YouTube, or your favorite podcast platforms.

Social media links:

FACEBOOK: @PHILCOOKEPAGE

TWITTER: @PHILCOOKE

INSTAGRAM: @PHILCOOKE

YOU HAVE A MESSAGE THAT NEEDS TO BE HEARD

It's time to innovate the way we package our message and bring it to market!

> "If I had Martijn in my life in my earlier years, my impact could have been greater. He has made my world larger and he can do the same for you."
>
> -Sam Chand